Year 9 Workbook

Published by Pearson Education Limited, 80 Strand, London, WC2R 0RL.
www.pearson.com/international-schools

Copies of official specifications for all Pearson Edexcel qualifications may be found on the website: https://qualifications.pearson.com

Text © Pearson Education Limited 2022
Project managed and edited by Just Content Limited
Designed and typeset by PDQ Digital Media Solutions Limited
Picture research by Straive
Original illustrations © Pearson Education Limited 2022
Cover design © Pearson Education Limited 2022

The right of Robert Greenhalgh to be identified as the author of this work has been asserted by him in accordance with the Copyright, Designs and Patents Act 1988.

First published 2022

25
10 9 8 7 6 5 4

British Library Cataloguing in Publication Data
A catalogue record for this book is available from the British Library

ISBN 978 1 292 39682 8

Copyright notice
All rights reserved. No part of this publication may be reproduced in any form or by any means (including photocopying or storing it in any medium by electronic means and whether or not transiently or incidentally to some other use of this publication) without the written permission of the copyright owner, except in accordance with the provisions of the Copyright, Designs and Patents Act 1988 or under the terms of a licence issued by the Copyright Licensing Agency, 5th Floor, Shackleton House, 4 Battlebridge Lane, London, SE1 2HX (www.cla.co.uk). Applications for the copyright owner's written permission should be addressed to the publisher.

Printed in Great Britain by Bell and Bain Ltd, Glasgow

Acknowledgements

Cover acknowledgements
Shutterstock: Janna7/Shutterstock 1

Text acknowledgements
Barack Obama: Quoted by President Obama 40; **Harper Collins:** Bearing the Cross: Martin Luther King Jr. and the Southern Christian Leadership Conference. (1986) p. 13. 14; **Infrapedia:** Global Internet Infrastructure Map by Infrapedia. https://www.infrapedia.com/app 156; **Penguin Random House:** Haskins, J., Haskins, J., Parks, R. (1999). Rosa Parks: My Story. United Kingdom: Puffin Books. 14; **Public Health England:** The mental health needs of gangaffiliated young people. Public Health England. 50; **Stockholm International Peace Research Institute:** Mission statement from SIPRI. Stockholm International Peace Research Institute 68; **Tim Berners-Lee:** Quote from Tim Berners-Lee webpage "Answers for Young People". 164; **TRAFFIC International:** What's Driving the Wildlife Trade? TRAFFIC International. 87; **United Nations:** United Nations Factsheet "Indigenous Peoples, Indigenous Voices. United Nations. Used with permission. 72.

Photo acknowledgements
123RF: prospective56/123RF 84; belikova/123RF 88; pytyczech/123RF 223; **Alamy:** PRISMA ARCHIVO/Alamy Stock Photo 202; **Shutterstock:** Oleksandr Molotkovych/Shutterstock 11; AlessandroBiascioli/Shutterstock 16; photka/Shutterstock 23; Aliaksei Tarasau/Shutterstock 61; Kzenon/Shutterstock 71; sirtravelalot/Shutterstock 71; Daniel Prudek/Shutterstock 80; Igor Podgorny/Shutterstock 82; Bill Florence/Shutterstock 88; holbox/Shutterstock 88; 2630ben/Shutterstock 92; Wyatt Rivard/Shutterstock 98; Bildagentur Zoonar GmbH/Shutterstock 98; Ricardo Reitmeyer/Shutterstock 101; RTimages/Shutterstock 106; 3DDock/Shutterstock 112; Andrey Kuzmin/Shutterstock 129; Jirsak/Shutterstock 184; THPStock/Shutterstock 10; Milan Adzic/Shutterstock 216; **PDQ Digital Media Solutions Ltd:** PDQ Digital Media Solutions Ltd/Pearson Education Ltd 172.

All other images © Pearson Education

Contents

Social Justice	9
Peace and Conflict	45
Sustainable Development	70
Identity and Diversity	131
Globalisation and Interdependence	155
Human Rights	201
Power and Governance	236
Glossary	259

Welcome to Global Citizenship!

We hope you will find this book useful as you approach the exciting subject of Global Citizenship! This book will form a key part of your journey to becoming a Global Citizen. It will help you understand the wider world, your place in it, how you can engage with issues locally and globally and how you can enact positive change.

Objective
This is what you will know or be able to do by the end of the session.

We will learn
This is what you will be learning in the session.

Key vocabulary
These are important words to know.

Information
This is an introduction to the session.

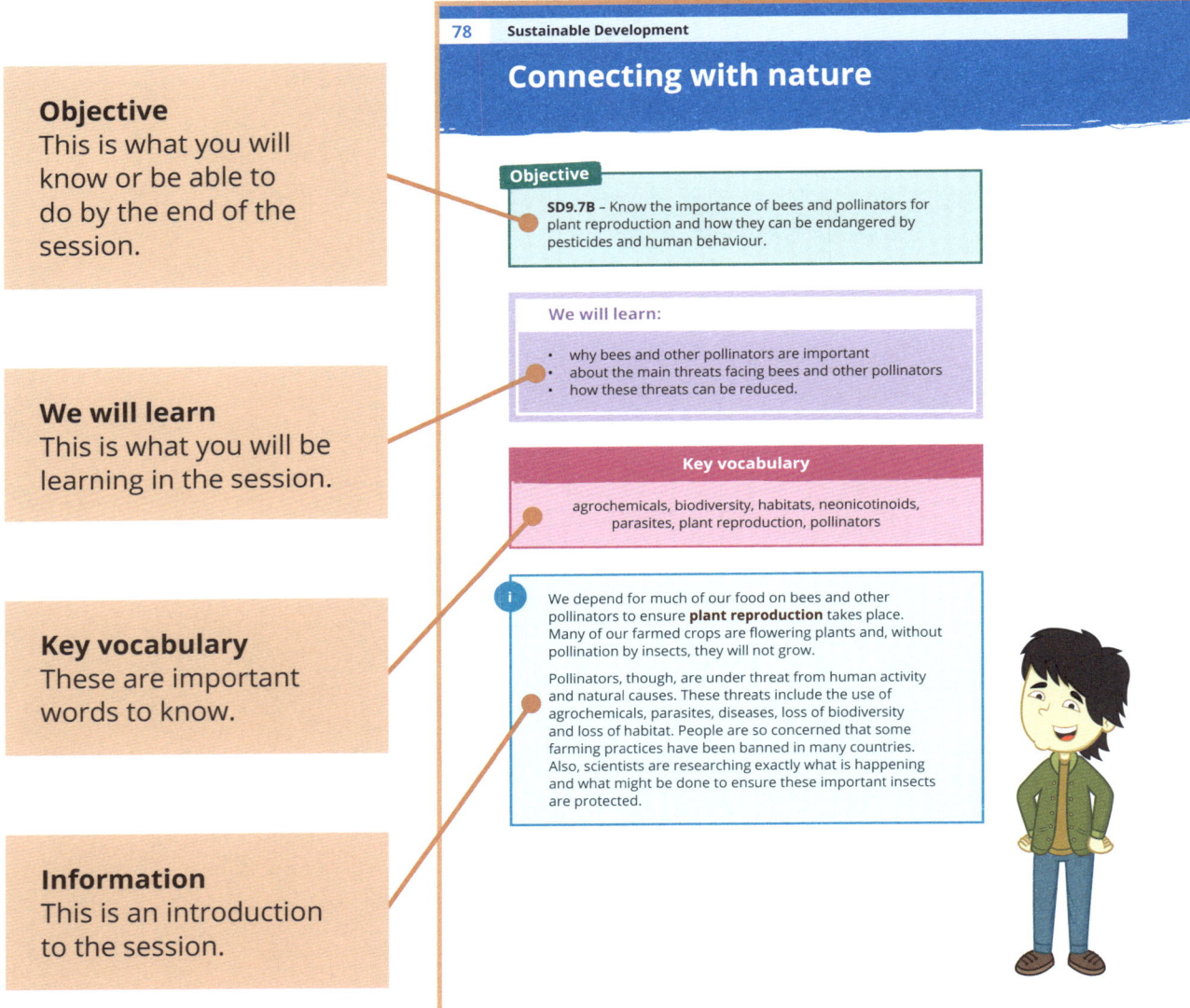

Introduction

This book provides a clear structure to your learning. Each unit is based around a Global Citizenship strand and clearly focuses on the mastery of key objectives. These objectives are set out at the start of each unit, along with the opportunity to reflect on what you have learned at the end of each session in the unit.

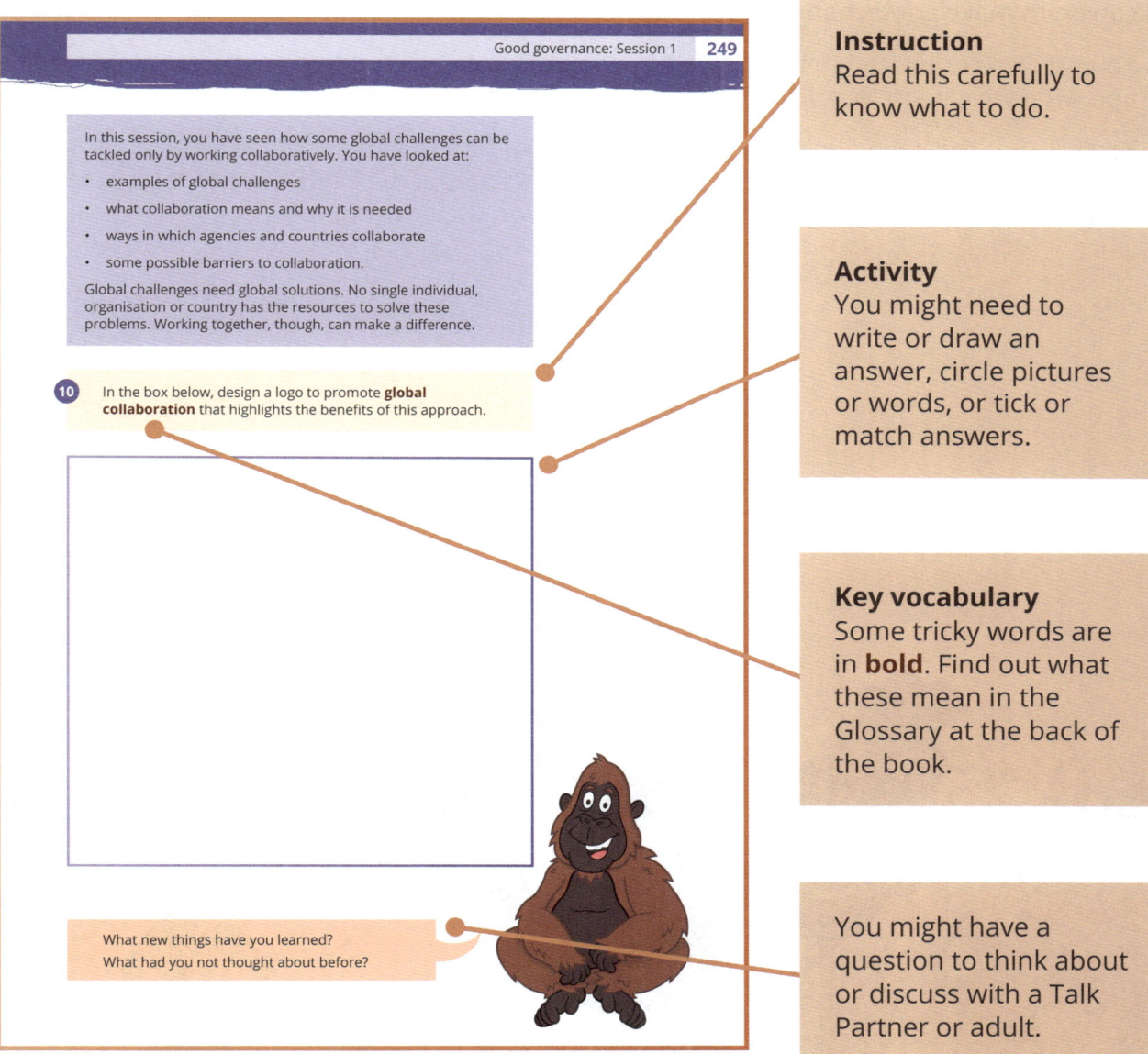

Instruction
Read this carefully to know what to do.

Activity
You might need to write or draw an answer, circle pictures or words, or tick or match answers.

Key vocabulary
Some tricky words are in **bold**. Find out what these mean in the Glossary at the back of the book.

You might have a question to think about or discuss with a Talk Partner or adult.

Meet the mascots!

Global Citizens!

We are all part of a Global Community – we are Global Citizens!

In this book you will meet lots of different people. Some may seem to be like you and some may seem to be different. However, everyone you meet will have something in common with you! Some may be from a part of the world you know, or from a city, town or village just like yours. You will discover how we are all part of a Global Community and that everything we do has effects on people, animals, and the wider world.

You will find that the same issues affect all of us. This book will help you learn what you can do to make good changes both locally and globally.

You will be encouraged to think about how our choices affect different groups of people and what we can do to help create a fairer world for everyone.

You will also meet, and learn about, some of the different animals which are also facing problems and may need our help. Many of these issues come from close contact with humans, or from the effect that people can have on the environment.

The Giant Panda

Giant Pandas now only live in China and are very rare, mainly due to the destruction of the bamboo forests they live in. Protecting their habitat also helps a lot of other animals and provides them with somewhere to live. Pandas are an excellent example of the different ways people can work to help animals.

The Malayan Tapir

Malayan Tapirs are found in parts of South-East Asia. Young tapirs are dark and have stripes to help them hide when they are young. Tapirs are at risk because of hunting and damage to their habitat caused by illegal logging. Although a protected species, their numbers are still declining.

The Golden Jackal

Golden Jackals live in parts of Africa and are quite common. Because there are so many of them and they can adapt to so many different environments, they often meet people and can be found near houses and farms. We need to learn how to live safely alongside this animal to avoid future conflict.

The African Elephant

The African Elephant is the world's largest land animal and can weigh as much as three family cars! Over many years, they have often been hunted by poachers and by farmers trying to protect their land from damage. These elephants can now use only one third of the land they could use 30 years ago. Now people are learning again about how to live alongside this giant.

The Sumatran Orangutan

The Sumatran Orangutan lives in the trees of tropical rainforests. The trees they live in are being cut down for wood and the land is used to grow other things which means they are very endangered. There are not many of these animals left now but organisations are trying to protect their forests and have established sanctuaries where they can live in safety.

Justice and injustice (Greater Depth)

Social Justice 9

Objective

SJE9.1A – Understand the legacy of colonisation, which made some people rich and caused exploitation and degradation to others.

We will learn:

- to understand what social justice is
- what colonisation means
- how colonisation created wealth for some but exploited and denied basic rights for others
- how colonisation in the past creates challenges today
- how the legacy of colonisation can be challenged
- how inequalities develop and how they can be addressed.

Key vocabulary

Atlantic slave trade, colonisation, discrimination, inequality, plantation, social justice, Triangular Trade

Social justice is concerned with how differences in ethnicity or gender, for example, lead to inequalities in wealth, opportunity and justice. Through the actions of individuals, organisations and states, people have been, and still are being, treated differently. This creates situations where some people profit and others suffer, and where the basic rights of some are denied. Often the causes are found many hundreds of years ago. One legacy of this is that many people living today are unaware that the discrimination found in the past still exists and continues to produce inequalities.

There is a need to challenge this and ensure that discrimination is addressed and equality of opportunity is accepted as a right that all people should have. This change can come about when individuals, organisations and states actively promote an understanding of the causes of discrimination and inequality, and take steps to find solutions.

The **Atlantic slave trade** took place from the sixteenth to nineteenth centuries, as European nations explored the world and embarked upon the **colonisation** of Africa, South and North America and the Caribbean. Colonisation means that a country claims the land of another people and, through political, economic and military means, controls the country and those already living there.

Settlers in the new colonies would create large agricultural estates, or plantations, and grow crops. These large plantations needed a regular supply of cheap labour and this was found by capturing and enslaving Black African people. African tribal chiefs and rulers would capture the enslaved people and were paid with items sent from Europe. These included guns, alcohol, textiles and other manufactured goods. The enslaved people were shipped across the Atlantic Ocean where they would be sold to slave traders or landowners and made to work on the plantations. The plantations produced raw materials that were in great demand in Europe, including sugar, cotton, tobacco, coffee, rum and cocoa. This three-way traffic in goods, enslaved people and raw materials became known as the **Triangular Trade**.

It is estimated that over 12 million Black African enslaved people – men, women and children – were shipped across the Atlantic Ocean. These enslaved people were kept in appalling conditions and treated very badly. Many died after being captured, either during the voyage or on the plantations.

1 Read the paragraphs opposite carefully. Draw **three** arrows on the map below showing how the movement of goods, enslaved people and raw materials formed the Triangular Trade of the Atlantic Ocean. Add labels to each side of the triangle to show what was being shipped.

Justice and injustice: Session 1

2 In the speech bubbles below are brief explanations of the part played by four people in the Atlantic slave trade. In each bubble, write 'P' if you think the person profited from the trade and 'E' if you think they were exploited by it.

Ship's captain
I command a trading ship and take enslaved people to America and raw cotton back to Liverpool in England. ☐

Tribal ruler
I rule a small tribe in West Africa and sell the enslaved people to a slave trader in return for things we do not have. ☐

Enslaved person
I was born on the **plantation**. Both of my parents are enslaved people taken from Africa. ☐

Banker
I lend money to businessmen. They use it to equip ships, buy cotton and build mills to turn the cotton into textiles. ☐

3 Think of **two** other people who profited from or were exploited by the Atlantic slave trade. Add details to the empty speech bubbles about who they were and what they did.

4 Who profited the most? Explain your choice.

_____
_____
_____

Justice and injustice: Session 1 | 13

By the mid-1800s, slavery had been abolished by most countries. However, this did not mean that the Black enslaved population became free and equal.

5 Explain the legacy of the Atlantic slave trade by selecting the correct words to complete the text below.

twentieth	opportunities	African	legalised
rights	transport	sporting	white
equality	schools	segregation	abolished

After slavery was _____, many former enslaved people were still made to work on plantations, and those that were freed did not have the same _____ and opportunities as the _____ population. Attempts were made to improve **social justice** and _____ – but these were not very successful.

By the early _____ century, _____ laws meant that, in the United States of America (USA) for example, African Americans were educated in different _____, could not share public _____ equally with white people and were prevented from taking part in major _____ events.

This _____ **discrimination** was widespread and affected most of the _____ American population, who found the _____ available to white people were not available to them.

From the 1950s, some individuals managed to challenge this discrimination. In 1955, for example, in Montgomery, USA, Rosa Parks refused to give up her seat to a white person travelling on the same bus. This was one act that led to the rise of the Civil Rights Movement in which Martin Luther King played an important role in the 1960s.

Martin Luther King promoted non-violent protest against the discrimination of African Americans, while other groups, for example Black Power and the Black Panther Party, were more militant and sometimes came into conflict with the police.

6 Read the two texts below. Text A is a summary of the regulations regarding segregation on buses in Montgomery, USA. Text B is taken from Rosa Parks' autobiography.

Having read the texts, look at the list of emotions on the opposiste page that some of the people involved in the Rosa Parks bus incident may have felt. Choose an emotion for each of the people listed and explain, in the space provided, why they might have felt that way. You can use the same emotion for more than one person.

Text A

'The first four rows of seats on each Montgomery bus were reserved for whites. Buses had "colored" sections for Black people generally in the rear of the bus, although Blacks composed more than 75% of the ridership. The sections were not fixed but were determined by placement of a movable sign. Black people could sit in the middle rows until the white section filled; if more whites needed seats, Blacks were to move to seats in the rear, stand, or, if there was no room, leave the bus. Black people could not sit across the aisle in the same row as white people. The driver could move the "colored" section sign, or remove it altogether. If white people were already sitting in the front, Black people had to board at the front to pay the fare, then disembark and reenter through the rear door.'

Text B

'People always say that I didn't give up my seat because I was tired, but that isn't true. I was not tired physically, or no more tired than I usually was at the end of a working day. I was not old, although some people have an image of me as being old then. I was forty-two. No, the only tired I was, was tired of giving in.'

Justice and injustice: Session 1 — 15

| angry | defiant | frightened | disgusted |

| embarrassed | calm | happy | frustrated |

Person	Emotion	Reason for this feeling
Bus driver		
White passenger		
Rosa Parks		

The case study of Rosa Parks is an example of institutionalised, legal discrimination. This means that people are treated differently simply because of, for example, their ethnicity, colour, age or gender. It is discrimination because it values one person above another. It is institutionalised because it is something that is part of the core beliefs and actions of an organisation or state. It is legal because laws or regulations have been passed that allow it to happen.

7 Look again at the case of Rosa Parks and complete the sentences below to explain why it is an example of institutionalised, legal discrimination.

1 It is institutionalised because _____

2 It is legal because _____

3 It is discrimination because _____

Recent developments in challenging discrimination include the rise of the Black Lives Matter movement. This started in 2013, after the acquittal of George Zimmerman following his shooting of Trayvon Martin. The circumstances reflect a number of high-profile cases in the USA where African Americans died after confrontations with the police.

In 2014, Laquan McDonald was killed by a police officer after refusing to drop a knife he was carrying. McDonald was walking away from the police officer and was shot 16 times. The police officer was found guilty of murder and was sentenced to 81 months in prison.

In 2020, George Floyd was killed after being held on the ground by police officers while one knelt on his neck. His death was followed by protests and demonstrations across the USA and worldwide.

Justice and injustice: Session 1 — 17

8 Look at the picture opposite of a Black Lives Matter protest. Using only evidence from the picture, indicate if you think the statements below are true, false or unknown. Add a tick for true, a cross for false and a question mark for unknown. In the final column, note what evidence you used to reach your conclusion.

Then add **three** statements of your own, together with a tick/cross/question mark and evidence, and answer the question below.

Statement	✓ ✗ ?	Evidence
The protest is taking place in the USA.		
The protest is peaceful.		
The protestors think racism is a positive thing.		
The protestors are all women.		
All the protestors are Black.		

What do you think could be some of the dangers of using a photo like the one opposite to draw conclusions about a situation? Think, for example, about what the photo doesn't show.

_____
_____
_____
_____

Justice and injustice: Session 1

The Atlantic slave trade not only resulted in the inhuman treatment of Black Africans but also established a legacy that continues to last long after slavery has been abolished.

There has been a growing awareness that this legacy has promoted deeply held prejudices that have, in turn, led to institutionalised, legal discrimination. The growth of the Civil Rights movement in the USA and the global growth of the Black Lives Matter movement have brought this into focus. People of all colours are realising that social injustice and **inequality** is a daily occurance for many people.

9 Explain the impact of colonisation on both those who were colonised and the coloniser. Give an example of how the legacy of colonisation has made an impact on your community.

_____
_____
_____
_____
_____
_____
_____
_____
_____
_____
_____
_____
_____
_____

What new things have you learned?
What had you not thought about before?

Wealth and poverty in society

Objective

SJE9.1B – Ability to critique the efficacy of initiatives, groups and individuals who are addressing poverty.

We will learn:

- what is meant by poverty
- how poverty is measured in the Global North and Global South
- how individuals, organisations and states view and combat poverty.

Key vocabulary

absolute poverty, poverty line, relative poverty, statistics

i   When we think of poverty, we tend to take a global view and focus on those parts of the world where poverty is commonplace. However, poverty does not respect geography. It is not confined to specific parts of the world but ranges far and wide. For example, during the COVID-19 pandemic, UNICEF funded the distribution of food parcels to hungry children in the United Kingdom.

Wealth and poverty in society: Session 2

Poverty is a wide-ranging term. We have some idea what it means, but the truth is that it means different things to different people. It can be useful to analyse different types of poverty to gain an insight into what it means for the people affected.

1 Draw lines to match these commonly used terms to their definitions.

absolute poverty	Children who are deprived of the material, spiritual and emotional resources needed to stay alive, develop and thrive
overall poverty	A higher than average proportion of a household income is spent on keeping warm, providing hot water and cooking
fuel poverty	Severe deprivation of basic human needs, including food, safe drinking water, sanitation facilities, health, shelter, education and information
child poverty	Not having enough income or material possessions to meet basic human needs
poverty	Lack of consistent access to enough food for an active, healthy life
food insecurity	Limited income and resources to ensure a sustainable and rewarding livelihood

Wealth and poverty in society: Session 2

One thing you will notice from Activity 1 is that the definitions are vague. To understand poverty more fully, you need to see how these definitions are interpreted by organisations and states.

2 Choose the correct words to complete the text which explains how the government of the United Kingdom (UK) measures poverty. You will need to read this carefully – not all the words are needed!

| fuel | children | food | Kingdom |

| poverty | line | absolute | insecurity |

In the United _____ , absolute _____ is defined as a household where the income is below 60 per cent of the median (middle) household income for 2010–2011 (adjusted over time for inflation). For 2020, a household income of less than £15,650 per year represented _____ poverty.

Relative poverty is defined as below 60 per cent of the median income of the year in question. Income is measured either before or after housing costs are deducted. The poverty _____ is where a household income is below 60 per cent after housing costs are deducted. For 2020, a household income of less than £17,760 per year represented relative poverty and was below the **poverty line**.

Child poverty is measured by how many _____ live in households below the poverty line.

Fuel poverty in the UK is defined as when a household's _____ costs are above the median level and were they to spend what is needed, they would be left with an income below the poverty line.

At the moment (as at 2021), there is no measure of food _____ in the UK, although one is planned.

22 Wealth and poverty in society: Session 2

3 Measuring poverty is complicated. Choose another state or organisation, and research how it measures poverty. Then answer the questions below.

1 Name of organisation or state:
_____

2 How is absolute poverty measured?
_____
_____

3 How is relative poverty measured?
_____
_____

4 How is the poverty line measured?
_____
_____

5 Why is it important to have very specific measures of poverty?
_____
_____
_____
_____

Wealth and poverty in society: Session 2

One of the main reasons for measuring poverty is to be able to compare different regions of a country or of the world. This allows people to determine where the most need is.

4 The table below shows some basic **statistics** regarding poverty in the UK. Research and find out similar statistics for another country or region of your choice, and complete the table. You may not be able to find all the statistics but the more you can find, the easier it will be to complete Activity 5. Use the empty statistics boxes to add statistics you might want to include.

Statistic	United Kingdom (UK)	_____
Poverty line	22 per cent of households, including 8 million adults, live below the poverty line.	
Child poverty	500,000 children go without three meals a day or fresh fruit and vegetables. In 2019, the UK government estimated that 4.2 million children were living below the poverty line. In 2020, 1 million children were eligible for free school meals.	
Food insecurity	8 million people struggle daily to eat. 4 million regularly go more than a day without food.	
Absolute/relative poverty	In 2018, this applied to 22 per cent of the population.	
Food banks	In 2008, 25,000 people used food banks. In 2019, that had risen to 1.9 million.	

5 You have been asked to produce an infographic for your school newspaper in which you compare the poverty of **two** countries or regions. Use the information about the UK and your research for Activity 4 to produce the infographic in the box below.

Remember that an infographic should use striking visuals and minimal text to convey information.

Wealth and poverty in society: Session 2

There are millions of people around the world who belong to a group known as 'the working poor'. These are people who, although they work, do not earn enough to meet their basic needs. According to the American Bureau of Labor Statistics, 6.3 million people were defined as the 'working poor' in the USA in 2019.

6 Research videos or articles for either the USA or a country or region of your choice using the search terms 'in work poverty' or 'the working poor'. Then compose a short email that you might send to your local people's representative. Your email should contain **two** paragraphs.

- Paragraph 1 should describe what life is like to be working but poor.
- Paragraph 2 should outline what you think should be done to make sure people who work have enough to live.

_____
_____
_____
_____
_____
_____
_____
_____
_____
_____
_____
_____
_____
_____
_____
_____
_____
_____

You have seen how important it is not just to measure and compare poverty but also to gain some understanding of the human impact of poverty.

In this activity, you will apply that knowledge by researching an initiative that aims to alleviate poverty.

7 You should research an initiative in a region of your choice and, on the page opposite, produce a short report that includes:

- a description of the programme or initiative
- the statistical measures that are guiding the programme
- at least one human-impact story
- at least one table, graphic or image
- your conclusion on how successful you feel the initiative has been.

You could choose a government programme, the work of a charity or other organisation, or even an individual trying to make a difference.

If you wish, you could make notes in the box below.

Wealth and poverty in society: Session 2

Report on _____

Wealth and poverty in society: Session 2

In this session, you have seen how poverty affects people around the world. You have seen that to combat poverty, it is necessary to develop methods of measuring it and to understand the facts and figures surrounding it, while also keeping sight of the human impact. Indeed, people will argue that poverty is not concerned with statistics but human stories.

Poverty is often about the choices people make – not of those who find themselves in poverty, since they have little choice, but of governments and organisations.

8 Write a checklist for measuring the success of an organisation, government or initiative in alleviating poverty. Include both statistical and human-impact measures.

- [ ] _____
- [ ] _____
- [ ] _____
- [ ] _____
- [ ] _____
- [ ] _____

What new things have you learned?
What had you not thought about before?

Equality of opportunity

Social Justice — 29

> **Objective**
>
> **SJE9.1C** – Know about some of the causes, impacts and complexities of global inequalities of opportunity and attempts to address them.

> **We will learn:**
>
> - what is meant by global inequalities of opportunity
> - about the causes of global inequalities of opportunity
> - about remedies to address the inequalities that exist.

> **Key vocabulary**
>
> global inequalities, global initiatives, Global North, Global South, systemic inequalities

> **i** It is a fact that there are global inequalities and that these inequalities cause problems. People who have all that they want or desire may not recognise that there are those who cannot fulfil these ambitions.
>
> The ambitions of people to live lives that are fulfilled are sometimes determined by their own actions but are most often determined by birthright, events, cultural norms or state policies over which they have no control.
>
> By the end of this session, will you decide that only individuals have the power for change? Or will you decide that individuals cannot change unless society recognises that inequalities are addressed by more than individual determination? Will you decide that there are **systemic inequalities** that require **global initiatives** to ensure that all people are treated equally and given equal opportunities?

Equality of opportunity: Session 3

1 What is inequality? What are the inequalities that exist in our modern world? Choose the correct words to complete the text below that explores these questions.

| girls | poverty | men | inequality |

| 7 billion | equality | Oxfam | wealth |

Inequality is a general term that needs more definition if we are to fully understand what is meant by it. For example, there are individuals whose _____ is over US $100 billion. According to Oxfam, the world's top 1 per cent richest people have twice as much wealth as the combined total wealth of nearly _____ of the poorest people.

There is also gender _____. For example, again according to _____, the 22 richest _____ in the world have more wealth than all the richest women in Africa.

However, it's not just about wealth but also other measures of _____. Each year, 100 million people are forced into extreme _____ because they cannot afford healthcare. One in five children will be denied education, of which the majority are _____.

Wherever we look and whatever measure is used, there are global inequalities that should be considered and addressed if we are truly to consider ourselves a global community.

2 Write your own definition of 'global inequality' below.

_____
_____
_____

3 Place a tick or a cross to show if you agree (tick) or disagree (cross) with the following statements regarding a range of **global inequalities**.

Statement	✓ ✗
Rich people are better than poor people.	
Men and women are treated unequally.	
Celebrities are better role models than non-celebrities.	
All ethnicities and ethnic groups are treated equally.	
People with a disability have the same opportunities as people without a disability.	
Some countries are better than others.	
People should be allowed to move freely between countries to find a better standard of living.	
Countries in the **Global North** have a duty to assist countries in the **Global South**.	
Inequalities in health, wealth and education will eventually disappear without outside intervention.	

4 From the statements above, select **one** that you strongly agree with and **one** that you strongly disagree with. Write out the statements and explain why you have chosen them.

Statement I strongly agree with: _____

_____

Reason: _____

_____

Statement I strongly disagree with: _____

_____

Reason: _____

_____

Equality of opportunity: Session 3

The causes of global inequalities of opportunity are complex. They may include cultural or social differences or beliefs; government policies; economic systems; or the forces of nature. The causes can lie both within and outside a country.

5 Draw lines to link the statements showing possible causes of inequalities of opportunity with their effect.

Cause	Effect
The government taxes everyone equally.	Talented people may be denied opportunities because they come from a background that limits their ambitions.
Climate change has caused a series of droughts leading to widespread famine.	Wealthy people keep their quality of life through the opportunities wealth brings. Poor people have less money to explore opportunities.
There is a rigid social structure with little mobility between classes.	Armed conflict displaces people from their homes and reduces time to seek opportunities.
There is a lack of strong government and armed conflict between warring factions is common.	Foreign aid builds opportunities through health, education and technology programmes.
Foreign governments cut their aid budgets.	Defence spending usually means income that could be used to improve opportunities is spent with overseas arms companies.
The government believes the country is threatened by surrounding countries and invests heavily in defence spending.	Extreme climate events have a significant impact on a country's resources and affect individuals opportunities to improve.

Equality of opportunity: Session 3

Inequalities of opportunity exist in both the Global North and the Global South, and there are many initiatives aimed at finding solutions. One such initiative is The Giving Pledge – a group of the most wealthy individuals use over 50 per cent of their wealth for the benefit of others. Founded in 2010, it now has over 200 'pledgers', each of whom are worth more than US $1 billion. The total amount pledged now exceeds US $800 billion.

6 Imagine you are a billionaire and have decided to join The Giving Pledge. Complete the pie chart to show how you will divide up your wealth. Divide it using percentages rather than amounts, and add labels or a key to show the specific charities or general programmes or aims to which you would like to donate money. If needed, research The Giving Pledge to see what initiatives individual billionaires are supporting.

Then answer the two questions that follow.

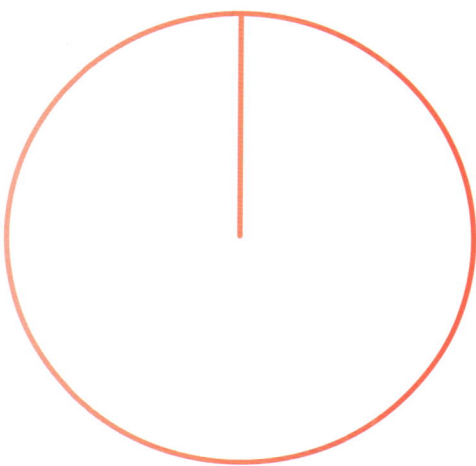

1 What are your reasons for distributing your wealth as shown in the pie chart?

_____
_____
_____
_____
_____

2 Why might billionaires want to give away over half their wealth?

_____
_____
_____
_____

7 It isn't always billionaires or large organisations that effect change to build opportunities out of inequality. Sometimes, an individual can make a difference, becoming a role model for others in the process. Read the story of one such individual and answer the questions that follow.

> Lala's family allowed her to attend school – unusual for a girl in her country. She continued her education, including English classes from charitable organisations, which led her to undertaking a journalism degree at university. Her online posts about her country's history caught the attention of a tour company. She became her country's first female tour guide.
>
> At first, Lala's parents were firmly against her plans to become a tour guide, since it was rare for a woman to work outside the home. She would also often face hostility from others who felt that a woman could not and should not work in this way.
>
> In the future, Lala aims to use her qualifications to work as a professional journalist as well as a guide. She wants to establish a tourism organisation for empowering female tour guides. She believes that tourism in her area will benefit from new guiding leaders with new perspectives, who have open minds and open hearts. She is determined to do her best to be an Agent of Change and an inspiration and role model for individuals facing similar challenges to those she has faced as a female tour guide and journalist.

1. What do you think were the main obstacles that could have prevented Lala from becoming a tour guide? For example, were these to do with gender, culture or religion?

   _____
   _____
   _____
   _____

2. What do you think were the key opportunities that Lala had that allowed her to become a tour guide?

   _____
   _____
   _____

3. Lala believes that change to provide opportunities will happen when guiding leaders have open hearts and minds. To what extent do you agree with this?

   _____
   _____
   _____
   _____

8 Research a story about either a billionaire or someone with more humble resources, like Lala, and how they have challenged inequality and provided or taken advantage of new opportunities.

Describe and explain your story using the headings provided.

Outline of story

_____
_____
_____
_____
_____
_____
_____
_____
_____
_____
_____

Reasons for choosing the story

_____
_____
_____
_____
_____
_____
_____
_____
_____
_____

Equality of opportunity: Session 3

In this session, you have looked at what is meant by global inequalities of opportunity and examples of these, together with their causes. You have explored initiatives that seek to correct these inequalities and provide opportunities for all. Some of these initiatives depend on extremely wealthy people, while others depend on the determination of much less wealthy people as they challenge the accepted view.

9 Give an example of a global inequality and explain how people have attempted to address it.

_____
_____
_____
_____
_____
_____
_____
_____
_____
_____
_____
_____
_____
_____

What new things have you learned?
What had you not thought about before?

Challenging injustice

> **Objective**
>
> **SJE9.1D** – Know that injustice has many roots such as ignorance, fear, misuse of power and overt discrimination, but that whatever its cause, it can be challenged.

We will learn:

- what is meant by injustice
- about the causes of injustice and the attitudes that may be part of these
- to use data to determine the effects of injustice
- some of the arguments used by those who deny injustice occurs or try to minimise its impact
- about the methods of challenging injustice.

Key vocabulary

Black Lives Matter (BLM), discrimination, injustice, institutionalised racism, micro-aggression, micro-discrimination, prejudice

> Most of us will experience some form of injustice; for some, it is a daily occurrence. However, being part of a local, national or global community means that we should all act to ensure injustice is challenged. Such challenges may aim to change an individual's behaviour, but in the case of institutionalised racism, for example, these challenges need to change the attitudes of whole groups of people or organisations.

Challenging injustice: Session 4

Column 2 in the table below shows how the total population of the United States of America (USA) is divided between different ethnicities. Column 3 shows how these same ethnicities are reflected in the prison population in the USA. The information is taken from the American Census.

Category	Population of USA	Prison population
Native American	1.5%	1%
Asian	5.9%	<1%
Hispanic/Latino	18.3%	19%
Black/African American	13.4%	40%
White	60.4%	39%

You might expect that the prison population would reflect the population as a whole, but there are two striking differences: 40 per cent of the prison population is Black, but only 13.4 per cent of the total population is Black; on the other hand, only 39 per cent of the prison population is white, yet 60.4 per cent of the total population is white. What does this mean?

1 Having read the information above, answer the questions below.

1 Why do you think the percentage of Black people in prison is higher than the percentage of Black people in the country? What could explain this imbalance?

_____
_____
_____
_____

2 What facts and statistics could you look up to support your ideas?

_____
_____
_____
_____

Challenging injustice: Session 4

In the first session of this topic, you looked at the legacy of the slave trade. Some people believe that part of this legacy is shown by organisations or institutions through racist actions or beliefs.

The international organisation **Black Lives Matter (BLM)** works to promote justice and raise awareness of **institutionalised racism**. Its mission is to expose and confront racism in the 'state', which includes governmental and justice systems.

2 Select the correct words to complete the text below about Black Lives Matter and institutionalised racism.

racist	**discrimination**	promotes	culture
institutionalised	few	challenged	BLM
white	Slave	Black	state

One of the core beliefs of the Black Lives Matter (_____) movement is that the _____ treats _____ people differently from other people. This is seen as part of the legacy of the Transatlantic _____ Trade. Enslaved people were not considered to be people in the same way that white people were. Black people were denied the same rights and opportunities that _____ people had. BLM supporters, and many other people, believe that these rights are still being denied and that this _____ must be _____ .

Many believe that the way Black people are treated by the state does not represent just isolated cases involving a _____ officials but is an example of _____ racism. Institutionalised racism means that there is a _____ throughout an organisation that, at best, ignores _____ behaviour or, at worst, _____ it.

There are many individuals, groups and organisations that argue against the BLM movement. Some of the more extreme views are held by people regarded as 'white supremacists', who believe that white people are 'better' and that they should have rights and opportunities that are denied to others. They believe that discrimination is part of the natural order.

Some less extreme views still seem to reflect the legacy and discrimination of the slave trade. One such view is common on social media, on placards at demonstrations and in the mainstream media. It is: **ALL LIVES MATTER!**

This is an example of **micro-discrimination** or **micro-aggression**. No one can deny that all lives matter, but as former President Obama said:

"I think that the reason that the organizers used the phrase 'Black lives matter' was not because they were suggesting that no one else's lives matter; rather... there is a specific problem that is happening in the African American community that's not happening in other communities."

3 Read the analogy below of the burning house, a commonly used example to illustrate micro-discrimination. On the page opposite, draw a cartoon that explains why this illustrates that claiming that all lives matter misses the message behind the BLM movement.

The Burning House

There are three houses. Each house has a large garden all around it. One of the houses is on fire. The fire department arrives with three fire trucks. One turns its hoses on the burning house. The other two turn their hoses on the remaining two houses.

When questioned why they don't all turn their hoses on the burning house, since the others are not in danger, the fire crews answer that "all houses matter".

Challenging injustice: Session 4

Injustice can be challenged, but how? BLM acts mainly through peaceful protest and political lobbying. What other methods are there?

4 Draw lines to match the type of challenge with its description.

Type	Description
peaceful protest	Organisations such as youth or ethnic groups work to promote their cause within their own communities.
legal challenge	Individuals, groups and organisations try to influence elected officials.
community programme	Laws that are seen as unjust are challenged in the courts. Criminal or civil cases are brought where there is evidence of wrongdoing or injustice.
individual intervention	An individual stands for election to local or national government with the aim of challenging an injustice.
political appointment	An individual is witness to discrimination and intervenes to stop it.
civil disobedience	Individuals, groups and organisations engage in a non-violent refusal to obey certain laws or governmental orders where these laws or orders conflict with the beliefs of those concerned.

It is not enough to challenge just the behaviour of individuals; the causes of the behaviour must also be understood. These causes may include ignorance, fear and misuse of power. These create **prejudice** in individuals, which means they believe they have the right to discriminate against other people or groups.

5 Research an **injustice** and use the space below to produce a short report or article, or an infographic, that outlines the causes of that injustice and explains how knowing the causes can lead to more effective challenges. This session has looked mainly at racism but you could consider injustice concerning gender, political views or disability.

Challenging injustice: Session 4

In this session, you have explored the nature of injustice through examining the BLM movement. You have seen that using data can help describe and explain when an injustice has occurred, and that by, discovering the causes, effective challenges can be made. These challenges may be directed towards individuals, whole groups or organisations.

We should be aware that people or groups who deny those injustices will also use methods to normalise injustice, sometimes to the point where it can be regarded as acceptable or even natural.

6 Give an example of a local injustice in your community. Say why you think this injustice exists and what can be done to challenge it.

_____
_____
_____
_____
_____
_____
_____
_____
_____
_____
_____
_____
_____
_____
_____

What new things have you learned?
What had you not thought about before?

Conflicts in the community

> **Objective**
>
> **PC9.4A** – Know about some education programmes to help children who have become involved with violence to choose a different path.

We will learn:

- how young people become involved in street gangs
- about the dangers of gang membership
- about organisations that help young people move out of gangs and change their often violent lives for a more rewarding future.

Key vocabulary

criminal activity, public health, street gangs

i Street gangs exist in most major cities across the world. In London in the UK, alone, there are over 200 gangs, with as many as 10,000 young people involved in some way or other. The Federal Bureau of Investigation (FBI) estimates that over 33,000 gangs operate in cities across the USA.

Young people are drawn into street gangs often at an early age and for a number of reasons. Once involved in a violent and criminal world, it can be very difficult to leave it behind.

The traditional response has been to target the criminal activities and to heavily police gang-related areas and people. In addition, and more recently, the 'public health' approach has been successful. For example in Scotland, there has been a dramatic decrease in gang-related activity using this strategy.

Conflicts in the community: Session 1

There are many different types of gang: criminal gangs, prison gangs and taggers are some examples. **Street gangs** differ to these and other types of gang.

1 Choose the correct words to complete the text below about street gangs.

| 90 | crime | drug | criminal |

| decreasing | territory | geographical | tags |

| characteristics | gangs | prison | street gang |

There is no universal definition of a _____.

Some names of types of gang are self-explanatory:

_____ gangs, motorcycle _____,

for example. Other common types include taggers, who

use graffiti, or _____, to mark their

_____.

Most street gangs share similar _____ and are

often found in one _____ area.

There is growing concern over the involvement of street gangs in

_____ activity, particularly _____

related, and also the violent nature of gang warfare. Knife

_____ in the UK is steadily increasing, although

the number of deaths is _____. In the USA, gun

crime is more common and over _____ per cent

of deaths in the 15 to 24-year-old age group is due to firearms.

2 Defining a street gang is difficult, but different gangs do share common characteristics. From the list below, tick those characteristics that you think are typical of street gangs.

Gang characteristics	Tick if found in street gangs
Members share something in common, for example, locality	
Common identifying marks, clothing, hand signals	
Wide age range but usually from early teens to late twenties	
Involved in crime	
Members regard themselves as part of a gang	
Some form of initiation to joining the gang	
A hierarchy or structure to the gang	
May include male and female members	
Has a name known to its members and other gangs	
Claims 'ownership' of turf (territory)	

Conflicts in the community: Session 1

3 Listed below are 12 common reasons that are given for young people becoming involved with street gangs. Rank them in order from 1 to 12, 1 being the most likely reason that might tempt people to become involved, 12 being the least likely reason.

Then answer the questions below.

Reason	Rank
For protection from other gangs or people	
Peer pressure	
Boredom	
To gain status	
Gangs are common in their area	
Lack of family support	
Financial reward	
Intimidation or threats	
A sibling is a member	
Lack of positive role models	
To feel part of a family	
To be part of a cultural identity	

1   How did you decide which reason to rank as number 1?

_____

_____

_____

2   How did you decide which reason to rank as number 12?

_____

_____

_____

Conflicts in the community: Session 1   49

4 Research stories told by gang members explaining how they got involved in a street gang. Then use the information you researched and the reasons listed in Activity 3 to answer the question below.

Present your answer in the form of a flow diagram, showing the typical route or sequence of events that might lead to someone becoming a street gang member. You may not need all the boxes given.

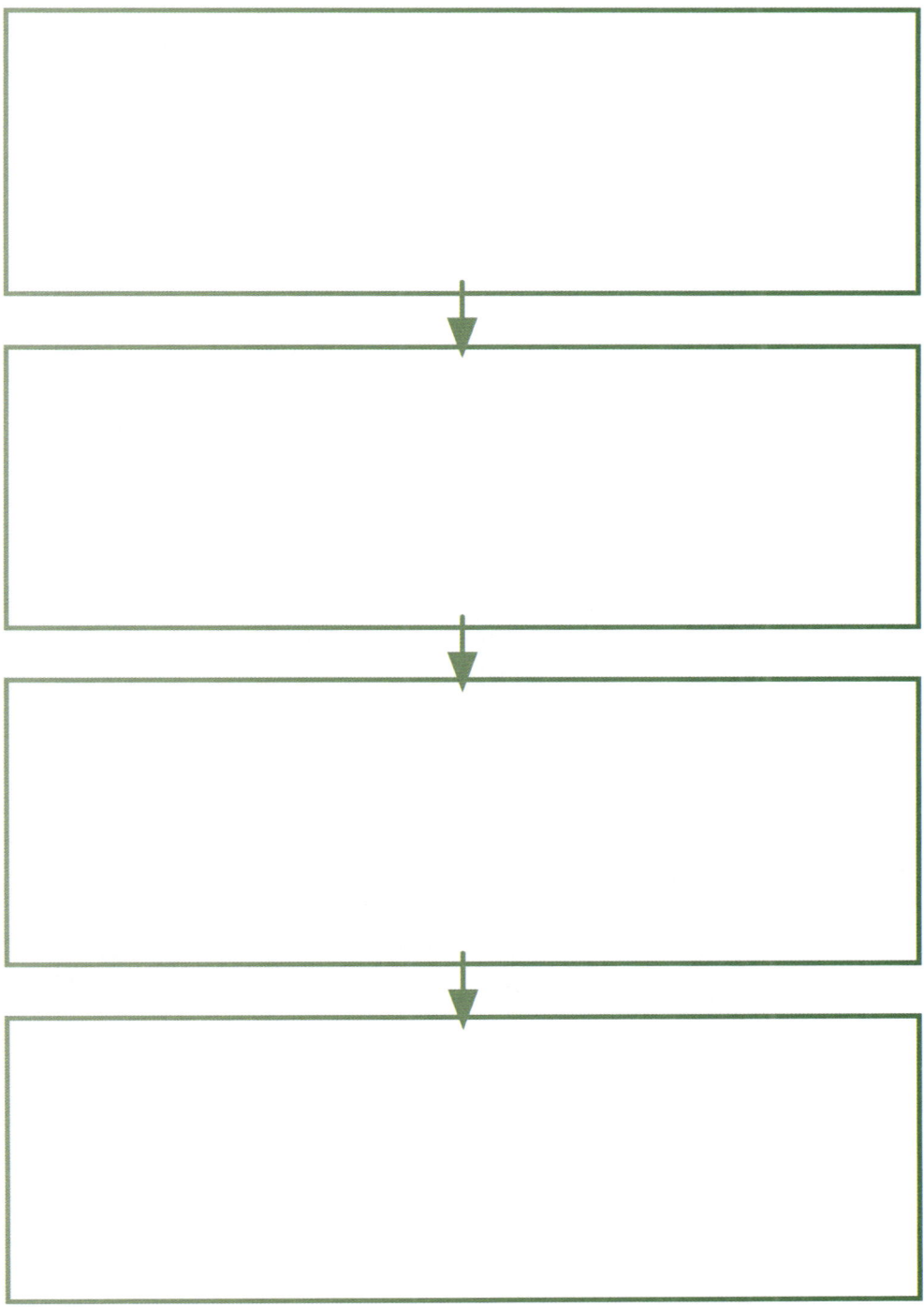

50 Conflicts in the community: Session 1

The effects of being a member of a street gang can be serious and long-lasting. We know that, apart from physical injury, mental health issues are common.

5 Look at the graph below. It shows the frequency of mental health problems in males who were or are gang members. Then answer the questions on the opposite page.

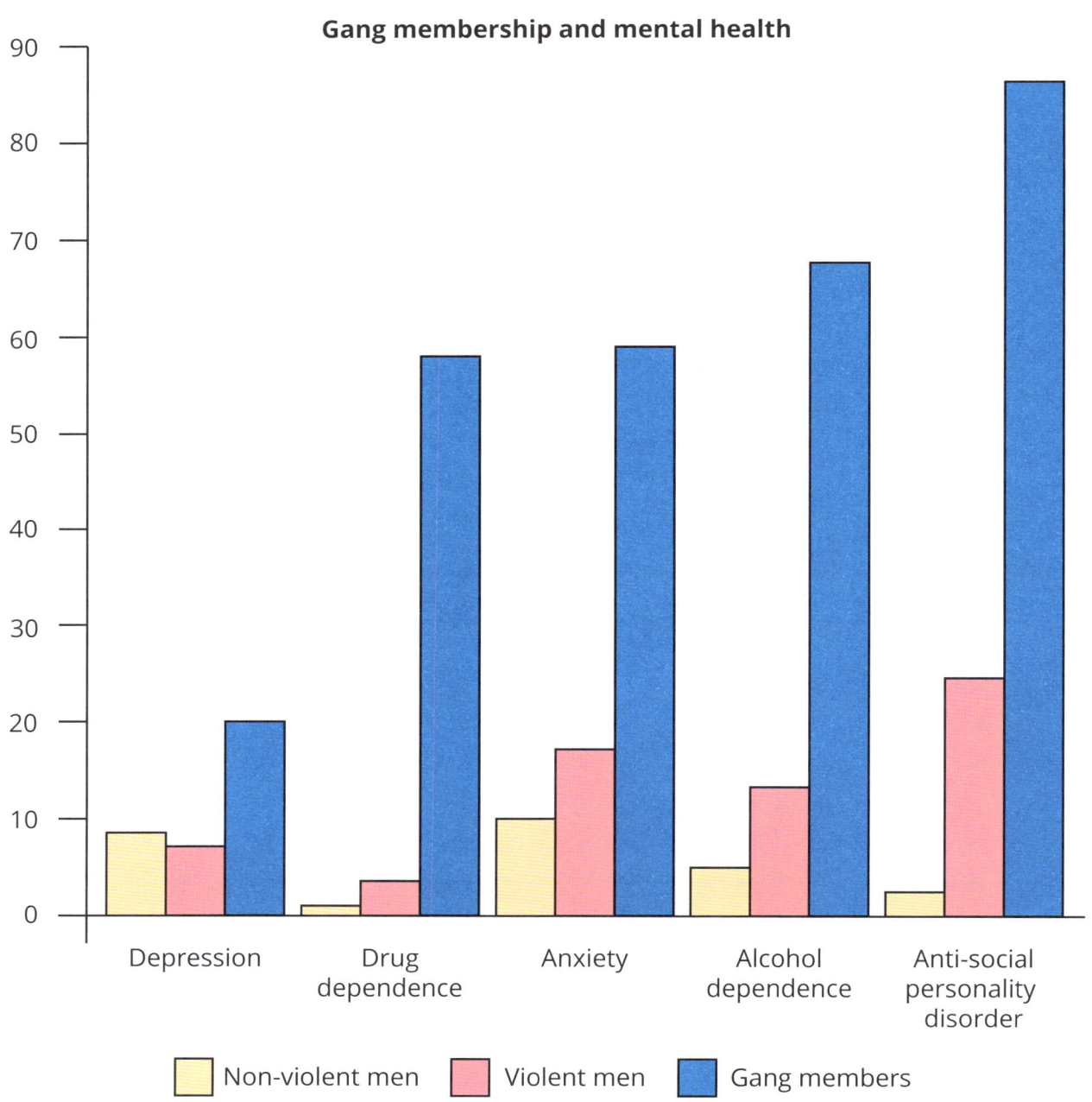

Gang membership and mental health

Non-violent men — Violent men — Gang members

1. Using information from the graph opposite, what percentage of gang members suffer from anti-social personality disorder?

   _____

2. Using information from the graph opposite, how much more likely is it that a gang member will be alcohol-dependent compared to a non-violent male?

   _____

3. Why do you think gang members are more likely to be drug-dependent?

   _____
   _____

4. Why do you think gang members are more likely to suffer from anxiety?

   _____
   _____

5. Do you think gang members are more likely to have these mental health issues **before** they join a gang or develop them **because** they join a gang? Give reasons for your answer.

   _____
   _____
   _____

6. Think of **three** reasons why leaving a gang might be difficult. Explain your answers.

Reason 1
_____
_____
_____

Reason 2
_____
_____
_____

Reason 3
_____
_____
_____

> Traditionally, street gangs were the subject of robust policing to reduce their influence and curb their criminal activities. In some cases, this is still a tactic that is used successfully.
>
> However, across the world, other methods are being used. Organisations have become involved, with the aims of helping people deal with the issues that promote gang culture and of showing gang members that life without a gang is better and safer than being in a gang. Often, former gang members are involved in such programmes.

7 Research methods and organisations that aim to address the root causes of street gang culture and help people to find an alternative to gang life. Use the following search terms to guide your research:

'Weed and seed strategy for combatting gang culture'
This is a strategy used in the USA. It involves police services 'weeding out' the most serious crime elements while at the same time 'seeding' neighbourhoods with rejuvenation and other community-based programmes to end gang dependency.

'The public health approach to reducing gang violence'
This approach, used in the United Kingdom and elsewhere, coordinates local councils, community leaders, schools and youth organisations to identity the risks and develop programmes to address the causes of gang violence.

Once you have researched, using text and videos, prepare an infographic on the opposite page explaining how you would tackle gang culture.

Conflicts in the community: Session 1

In this session, you have explored how young people can be drawn into street gangs and the culture of **criminal activity** and violence that come with them. If gang members avoid prison or physical violence, living in constant fear may cause significant mental health issues that remain with them for a long time.

There are organisations and agencies that are working to address, not just the criminal aspects of gang culture, but also the social and economic causes. The effects of some programmes has seen a significant reduction in gang activity in general and violent injury in particular.

8 Write an eight-line poem that describes how a young person who has become involved in violence can break the cycle and choose a different path, to live a better life. Give your poem a title.

What new things have you learned?
What had you not thought about before?

Resolving conflicts peacefully

Objective

PC9.4B – Know about how some serious conflicts in the past have been resolved peacefully.

We will learn:

- what is meant by a 'peaceful resolution'
- about the organisations involved in conflict resolution
- about some examples of conflict resolution.

Key vocabulary

armed conflict, Cold War, conflict resolution, peacebuilding, peacekeeping, war

At any point in time, there are up to 50 serious armed conflicts occurring around the world. In 2020, over 100,000 United Nations peacekeepers were deployed on 12 missions, mainly in North Africa and the Middle East.

How do these conflicts end? We tend to think wars end when one side surrenders. The examples of the First and Second World Wars helped to shape this perception. The reality is quite different. Most conflicts end when all the groups involved realise it needs to end!

In this session, you will look at examples showing the nature of armed conflict, how it ends and what steps can be taken either to prevent conflict starting in the first place or to maintain peace once conflict has ended.

Resolving conflicts peacefully: Session 2

1 What is a **war**? What is a proxy war? Draw lines to match the words or phrases to their correct definitions.

war	When the state engages in military operations against one or more armed groups within its own borders. Used to be called 'civil war'.
proxy war	When two or more states or countries avoid war directly between themselves but support other warring groups. These groups engage in **armed conflict** in countries that are not governed by the major states.
armed conflict	A general term, no longer used, to describe armed conflict.
internal armed conflict	When an outside agency, for example, the United Nations, ensures opposing groups do not revert to armed conflict.
international armed conflict	When armed groups, countries or states engage in military operations against each other. Used to be called 'war'.
peacekeeping	When military operations are carried out between states or countries. Has also replaced the term 'war'.
peacebuilding	When action is taken by an outside agency to reduce tensions between armed groups that might otherwise result in conflict.
Cold War	A particular period when the superpowers – primarily the Union of Soviet Socialist Republics (USSR) and the USA – amassed a large nuclear arsenal.

Resolving conflicts peacefully: Session 2 — 57

2 Few armed conflicts end with one side surrendering and the other being victorious. Select the correct words to complete the text below about ending conflict, and then answer the question that follows.

| Japan | armistice | international | conflict |
| ceasefire | armed conflicts | hostilities | Second |

The _____ World War ended with Germany, _____ and Italy being forced to surrender because of overwhelming military force. The First World War, though, ended with an _____ in which both sides agreed to stop fighting. It is more common for modern _____ to end in a _____ rather than a surrender. For this to be successful, all the parties have to agree, and _____ peacekeepers may have to ensure the ceasefire holds.

It is also important that whatever caused the _____ is addressed, otherwise _____ may start again.

Why do you think most armed conflicts end in a negotiated peace rather than one side trying to force the other to surrender? Think about the human and economic cost of conflict and also the influence of other states.

_____
_____
_____
_____
_____
_____

Resolving conflicts peacefully: Session 2

Sometimes, although conflict seems likely, it doesn't happen. The Cold War is an example of a potential conflict, where open warfare between the most powerful nations was avoided.

The Second World War ended when the USA dropped nuclear bombs on Hiroshima and Nagasaki, forcing the unconditional surrender of Japan. The Soviet Union and the USA then embarked on an 'arms race' in which they and their allies developed nuclear weapons to ensure they could match each other in the event of conflict. Their expanding nuclear arsenals of missiles, aircraft and submarines soon meant that any conflict would be so devastating that people seriously believed the human race could be annihilated. The phrase 'mutually assured destruction' was used to describe a conflict that, if started, would result in complete destruction.

A series of arms-limitation talks took place to reduce the size of the nuclear capabilities of all concerned. Through these negotiations, the number of warheads has fallen from over 70,000 in 1986 to under 14,000 today. However, the concerns remain because more countries now own nuclear weapons or are trying to develop them, and there is still the potential to cause destruction on an unimaginable scale.

The Cold War, though, remains an example of a conflict avoided through diplomacy, public opinion and the certainty of – and the need to avoid – destruction on all sides.

3 Use the information above and your own research on the Cold War to produce, on the opposite page, an article for your school magazine. Use the box below to make notes.

Explain how (and why) peace was maintained even though the global powers were deeply distrustful of one another and had weaponry. Include at least one diagram or illustration in your article, which will also need a title.

Resolving conflicts peacefully: Session 2

The United Nations devotes considerable resources to **conflict resolution**. At any one time, there may be over 100,000 peacekeepers engaged on missions to prevent warring parties resorting to armed conflict. They do this through two types of programme.

Peacebuilding is about dealing with the reasons why people fight in the first place, and supporting societies to manage their differences and conflicts without resorting to violence. Peacebuilding can take place before, during or after a conflict and can include:

- disarming potential combatants
- integrating combatants into society
- building/rebuilding infrastructure (roads, communications)
- building/rebuilding utilities (power, water)
- trauma counselling
- justice and restoration.

Peacekeeping is about using military personnel to enforce a truce or ceasefire between hostile states or communities. It takes place once armed conflict occurs and when all parties have agreed to stop fighting. Peacekeeping can involve:

- maintaining peace and security
- protecting civilians
- disarming combatants
- promoting rights
- restoring the rule of law.

4 Using the information above, and your own research on peacebuilding and peacekeeping, complete the table below to show what you think are **two** advantages and **two** disadvantages of each approach.

Peacebuilding	Peacekeeping
Advantages 1 _____ _____ 2 _____ _____	Advantages 1 _____ _____ 2 _____ _____
Disadvantages 1 _____ _____ 2 _____ _____	Disadvantages 1 _____ _____ 2 _____ _____

Resolving conflicts peacefully: Session 2 — 61

5 The United Nations has many current peacekeeping missions. With guidance from your teacher, do some online research into a current peacekeeping operation of your choice. Then answer the questions below.

1 Where is the peacekeeping mission located?
_____

2 How long has the peacekeeping mission been active?
_____

3 In your own words, describe the main reasons for the peacekeeping mission and the intended objective.
_____
_____
_____
_____
_____
_____
_____
_____
_____
_____
_____
_____
_____
_____
_____
_____
_____
_____
_____
_____

Resolving conflicts peacefully: Session 2

> Peacekeeping is not just carried out by the United Nations. Individual states take unilateral (on their own), bilateral (with another state) or multilateral (with several other states) action to intervene in conflict zones around the world. Conflict resolution is complex. There is no one solution.

6 Imagine you are given the task of creating a conflict resolution task force. The role of your task force is to:

1. prevent armed conflict occurring, where possible
2. intervene on the ground to stop warring parties fighting
3. ensure a lasting peace between the parties.

Under the headings below, list the **three** main elements or components of your task force, and explain their roles. You could include, for example, negotiators, **military equipment** and personnel, and humanitarian aid specialists.

Element 1

_____
_____
_____
_____

Element 2

_____
_____
_____
_____

Element 3

_____
_____
_____
_____

Armed conflict is common enough in the world for it to be a major concern. The fact that most armed conflicts end up in a stalemate, where neither side can win, does not deter groups or states from embarking on this destructive course of action.

There are organisations, such as the United Nations, with a proven track record in conflict resolution, and other organisations, states or individuals have shown a willingness, for whatever reason, to also intervene.

From the examples you have studied, you will have seen that direct, armed intervention rarely succeeds in stopping conflicts unless there is a willingness for all parties to cease hostilities and seek a political solution.

7 Give an example of a historical conflict that was resolved peacefully. Explain how this was achieved.

_____
_____
_____
_____
_____
_____
_____
_____
_____
_____
_____
_____
_____

What new things have you learned?
What had you not thought about before?

Conflicts around the world

Objective

PC9.4C – Know about the remit and reach of defence and security companies and their role in global peace and conflict.

We will learn:

- about the scale of the defence and security industry
- about the economic, political and ethical aspects of the global arms trade
- about both sides of the argument as to whether arms sales are necessary or desirable.

Key vocabulary

arms trade, defence, global arms sales, military equipment, security

The arms and security industry is a big business. In 2019, sales of **military equipment** and services accounted for well over US $360 billion, an increase of over 8 per cent on the previous year. Estimates vary, but, in the USA, over 1 million people work directly or indirectly in the defence industries. According to the World Bank, there are over 25 million military personnel in the world's armed forces, supplied mainly by the top 25 companies and the leading six or seven countries.

A single bullet may cost as little as US $0.25 but several million may be used in a single conflict. US $9.8 billion will buy a CVN-78 Class aircraft carrier. Preparing for conflict is an expensive business, exceeded only by the cost of actual conflicts when the cost in human suffering and economic destruction is added to the material cost of weapons and military equipment.

Conflicts around the world: Session 3   65

The reach of the arms industry is controversial. The sale of arms is seen by many as a valid form of trade, and there is a strong argument that arming nation states to defend themselves against aggression is not only reasonable but expected.

However, there is a point where **defence** of a nation state merges into providing arms for an immoral purpose. This is where you will need to decide how you feel about the global **arms trade**.

The economics of being a major arms provider are without question: it is a valuable source of income. But we need to balance against that the cost in human suffering.

1 Select words to complete the text below, which outlines both sides of the argument.

| development | profit | defence | aggression | legitimate |

| functions | nations | conflict | weapons | human |

Most people would agree that defending their 'territory' against armed _____ is a good thing. It is one of the _____ of a government to provide for the **security** of its people. In order to do this, many nation states have invested heavily in building an arms industry to supply their need for _____ .

But we live in a commercial world, and developing new weapons can cost billions. If no one nation state can provide enough orders to support the _____ of _____ weapons, then overseas sales have to provide the _____ that is expected.

Most concern is raised when those overseas sales are not used for defence but _____ – to engage in conflict against another state. The _____ cost of this can be devastating.

Many would argue that allowing arms manufacturers to sell weapons to other _____ is wrong. Others would see this as a _____ trade.

Conflicts around the world: Session 3

2 In each speech bubble, place a tick in the box if you think the opinion supports the global arms trade, a cross if it condemns the global arms trade and a question mark if it neither supports nor condemns it. Then answer the questions below.

Opinion 1
I and thousands of others work in the arms industry, pay taxes and defend our country. ☐

Opinion 2
Selling arms to oppressive regimes is just wrong. ☐

Opinion 3
Why not sell arms to our allies? After all, they are fighting the same battles we are. ☐

Opinion 4
If we spent as much money on tackling global inequalities as we do on arms, the world would be a better place. ☐

Opinion 5
If we don't sell them the arms, someone else will. ☐

Opinion 6
Selling arms for defence is one thing; selling them to violate rights is another. ☐

1 Which of the opinions do you most identify with? Give a reason.
_____
_____
_____

2 Which of the opinions do you least identify with? Give a reason.
_____
_____
_____

3 What other argument can you make for agreeing with the global arms trade?
_____
_____
_____

4 What other argument can you make for disagreeing with the global arms trade?
_____
_____
_____

Conflicts around the world: Session 3   67

3 Look at this list of reasons that defence and security companies might give to justify their sale of arms. Rank them from 0 to 5 according to how convincing you find them: 0 = not very convincing; 5 = very convincing.

Reasons for selling arms	How convincing (0–5)
Many of the weapons are sold to the armies of stable and responsible states.	
Many of the arms sold are not used in humanitarian and rights abuses.	
States have the right to use arms to protect the life and liberty of their citizens against attack.	
Arms play an important role in international peacekeeping operations.	
The arms industry offers employment to thousands of people.	

4 A number of organisations are opposed to the global arms trade. Listed below are some of the facts they use in their campaigns. As with Activity 3, rank these from 0 to 5 according to how convincing you find them: 0 = not very convincing; 5 = very convincing.

Reasons to oppose the sale of arms	How convincing (0–5)
Some weapons go to countries where they are used for humanitarian and rights abuses.	
90 per cent of people killed in armed conflicts are civilians.	
Money that is spent on buying arms could be better used on health and education and preventing poverty.	
The sale of arms promotes violence as an accepted way of resolving differences.	
One person dies every minute from armed violence – in that same minute, 15 new weapons are made.	

Conflicts around the world: Session 3

There are a number of organisations around the world that campaign to end the global arms trade. The Stockholm International Peace Research Institute (SIPRI) is based in Sweden. On its website it lists its aims as:

- undertake research and activities on security, conflict and peace
- provide policy analysis and recommendations
- facilitate dialogue and build capacities
- promote transparency and accountability
- deliver authoritative information to global audiences.

5 In the box below, design a logo for the SIPRI that communicates its aims, in a visual way, to the public. You could choose to focus on one, some or all of the aims listed above.

Conflicts around the world: Session 3   69

While many agree that a strong military is essential for home defence, many question the sale of arms to countries that may use the weapons not just to defend themselves but to carry out aggression against other states.

Some would argue that, without state support of **global arms sales**, the humanitarian suffering caused by armed conflict would be greatly reduced. Others argue that conflict is part of being human and supplying arms to support this is therefore a natural business opportunity. Have you reached an opinion as to whether the arms trade is essentially a positive or negative thing?

6 In the diagram below, state your opinion and add your supporting reasons.

| Reason 1 | Reason 2 | Reason 3 |

My opinion is that _____
_____.

| Reason 4 | Reason 5 | Reason 6 |

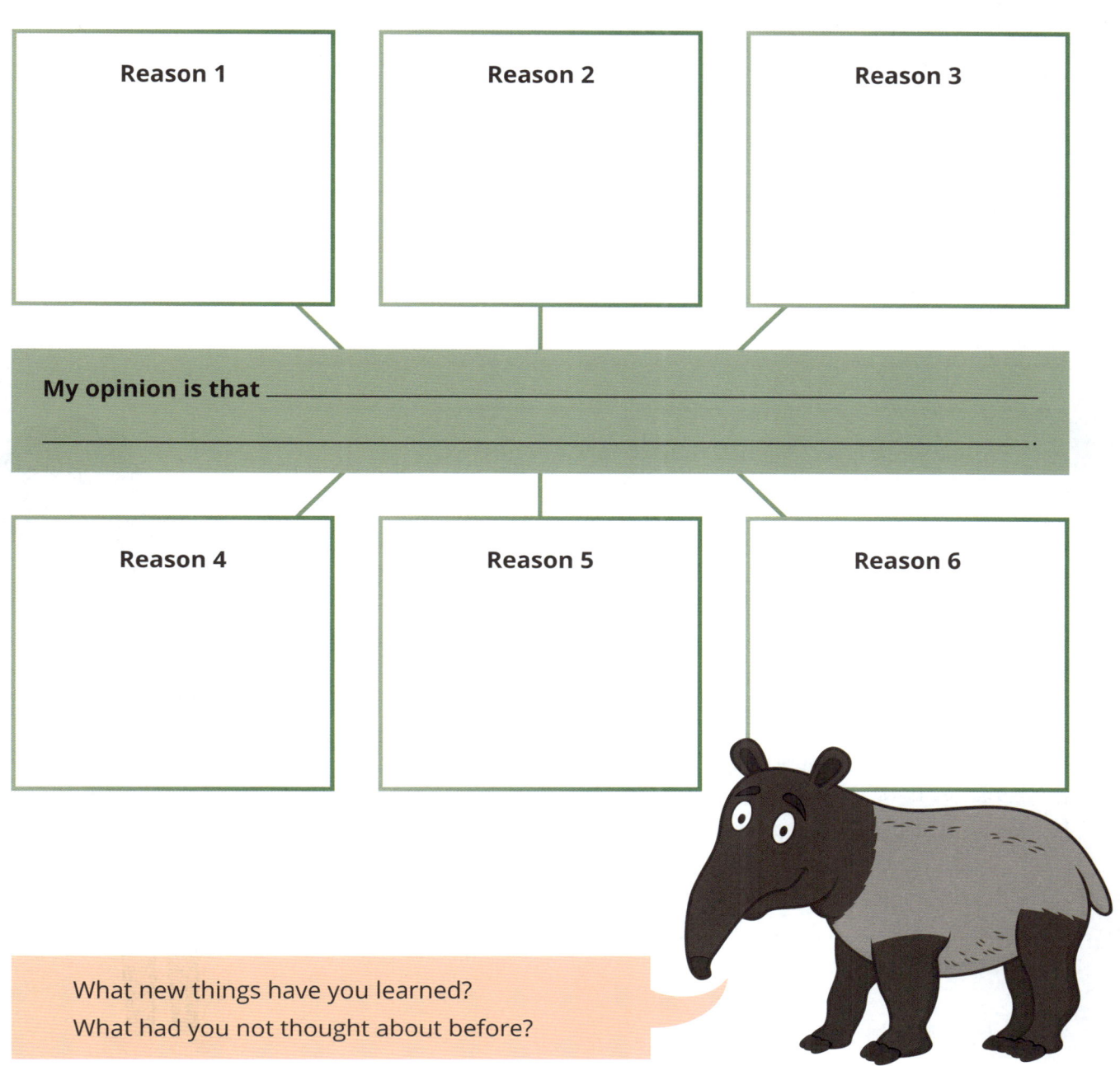

What new things have you learned?
What had you not thought about before?

Sustainable Development

Planet Earth

> **Objective**
>
> **SD9.7A** – Ability to learn from First Nation and Indigenous peoples how to live in sustainable ways.

> **We will learn:**
>
> - who First Nation and Indigenous peoples are
> - about the different worldview of First Nation and Indigenous peoples
> - how relevant this worldview is to the 'Western world' and particularly in relation to sustainability.

> **Key vocabulary**
>
> First Nations, Indigenous, sustainable, technology, worldview

ⓘ When there is a challenge that faces the world, we often look to technology to provide a solution. We build sea defences to protect our coastlines from flooding caused by the sea level rising. We race to find vaccines to combat viruses. These are two examples where Western technology is seen as the way forward. But what if there are alternatives?

In this session, you will explore how First Nation and Indigenous peoples regard such challenges and the technologies used to meet them. You will learn to question the purpose of technology and also our relationship with planet Earth.

There may be lessons we can learn from the wisdom of adopting a different worldview and developing and using technologies that are more sustainable.

Indigenous people can be described as people native to an area who are culturally and ethnically different from the colonisers and settlers who now make up the majority of the population. Their lands were often taken by European settlers.

There are approximately 400 million Indigenous people living in over 90 countries around the world. In some countries, a high proportion of their total population are Indigenous: for example, in Greenland, Indigenous people make up nearly 90 per cent of the population. There are, across planet Earth, well over 5,000 separate Indigenous cultures.

'**First Nations**' is a name given specifically to some Indigenous peoples of Canada that live as over 600 communities, representing about 4 per cent of Canada's total population. First Nations or First Peoples of Australia is also the preferred name for Aboriginal and Torres Strait Islanders in Australia.

1 Look at the table below. Research and find out about some more Indigenous peoples and add them to the empty rows.

Indigenous people	Main countries or areas
Inuit	Greenland
Lakota	North and South Dakota (USA)
Mayas	Guatemala
Aymaras	Bolivia
Uighurs	China
Aboriginal and Torres Strait Islanders	Australia
Maasai	Kenya and Tanzania (Africa)

Planet Earth: Session 1

'Indigenous peoples are the holders of unique languages, knowledge systems and beliefs and possess invaluable knowledge of practices for the **sustainable** management of natural resources. They have a special relation to and use of their traditional land. Their ancestral land has a fundamental importance for their collective physical and cultural survival as peoples. Indigenous peoples hold their own diverse concepts of development, based on their traditional values, visions, needs and priorities.'

The quote above gives some clues why we can learn from Indigenous peoples when finding solutions to some of the problems that face planet Earth.

2 Below are five proverbs that give some insight into the way many Indigenous peoples view planet Earth, or their worldview. Read them and answer the questions below.

> Treat the Earth well. It was not given to you by your parents; it was loaned to you by your children.

> We are all visitors to this time and place. We are passing through. We look, we learn, then we return home.

> A nation becomes great when old men plant trees whose shade they know they will never sit in.

> In the old days, you were measured not by how much money you had but how well you fed, sheltered and took care of your people.

> Let us put our minds together and see what life we can make for our children.

1 Two of the proverbs mention children. Why do you think that is?
   _____
   _____

2 What does the proverb about old men planting trees say about a nation achieving 'greatness'?
   _____
   _____

3 Why do you think Indigenous peoples identify with and respect the land?
   _____
   _____

Planet Earth: Session 1

Many Indigenous peoples have a particular way of looking at the world. They have a special bond with and a respect for the land. This **worldview** is reflected in how they believe the basic needs for food, shelter, water and energy should be met. The people serve the land; the land does not serve the people: this is one way they would describe their beliefs.

This worldview is reflected in Indigenous people's use of **technology**. To understand this, you need to consider first what technology is.

3 Select the correct words to complete the text below about technology.

Indigenous	sustainable	land	problems
with	Western	environmental	devices
knowledge	natural	science	solutions

Technology is about finding _____ to meet human needs. It differs from _____ , which is more concerned with understanding the workings of the _____ world. However, technology is also concerned with using scientific _____ for practical purposes.

Most people think of technology as the use of machines or _____ , but it is also concerned with finding new methods and systems to solve _____ .

Indigenous peoples, with their link to the _____ , have developed technological solutions to many _____ challenges. These often differ to ways in which _____ technology tackles the same problems and can provide solutions that are more _____ .

_____ technology offers a different approach in which solutions are not imposed on the land but which work _____ the land to meet our needs.

Indigenous technology offers alternative solutions to modern-day problems. Below are brief summaries of three examples of where traditional methods are proving more effective than Western technology.

Indigenous fire management in Australia

The devastating wildfires in Australia in 2019–20 destroyed millions of hectares of land and thousands of homes. They caused the deaths of over 30 people as well as countless numbers of wildlife. In order to prevent such severe fires in the future, people are looking at traditional Aboriginal methods of managing fires.

Drought-resistant plants and livestock in Burkina Faso

The advance of the Saharan desert is causing major problems for farmers in Burkina Faso. Modern methods of farming are not suited to the arid conditions. Instead, they are reviving Indigenous methods to combat the drought conditions.

Lima's pre-Incan water supply

Lima, Peru's capital city, is facing a water crisis. Climate change and desert conditions mean supplying water to its 10 million inhabitants is becoming increasingly difficult. The authorities are looking to ancient, pre-Incan canal systems to provide a reliable source of water.

4 Research the three examples above and complete the factsheet on the opposite page. Use the summary headings as online search terms to find information. For each example, your factsheet should include:
- at least one photograph, illustration or diagram
- a summary of the problem
- a description of the solution using Indigenous technology
- an explanation of why the Indigenous solution works.

Planet Earth: Session 1 — 75

Indigenous fire management in Australia

Drought-resistant plants and livestock in Burkina Faso

Lima's pre-Incan water supply

Planet Earth: Session 1

> Indigenous technology stems from a worldview in which the land plays an important part. There is a relationship between Indigenous peoples and the land that is less apparent with modern technology and lifestyles.

5 The statements below suggest reasons why some of us in more urban settings no longer connect with our environment. Put a tick against those statements you agree with and a cross against those you disagree with.

Statement	✓ ✗
People live in towns and cities of concrete and steel. There is no land to respect.	
Houses, shops and offices are designed to give control over their environment.	
A worldview of respect for the land is not compatible with modern lifestyles.	
Modern problems need modern technology, not ancient technology.	
Indigenous peoples live in close communities. That's not how most can live.	
If everyone adopted an Indigenous worldview, we would have to give up too much.	
Society has come too far to go back to an Indigenous worldview.	
Indigenous knowledge and skills are lost to most of us and cannot be regained.	

6 The editor of the school magazine would like to include the factsheet you produced for Activity 4 in the next edition. Write an introductory paragraph to the factsheet that puts the case for adopting a more Indigenous worldview and the use of appropriate Indigenous technology. You could use some of the statements from the previous activity, turning them into positive reasons.

_____
_____
_____
_____

In this session, you have explored what is different about the way Indigenous peoples view their environment, and how the technology they use reflects this worldview and sometimes offers a better solution to modern challenges than Western technology. Traditional skills and methods were developed to meet people's needs that also, out of respect for the land, provided a sustainable answer to the challenges they faced.

Today, the greatest challenge faced by planet Earth is climate change. There are many who think that, to find solutions, we need to work with our environment like the Indigenous peoples, rather than trying to force the land to meet our needs.

7 Choose a sustainable practice used by Indigenous peoples and explain how it can help to relieve climate change.

What new things have you learned?
What had you not thought about before?

Sustainable Development

Connecting with nature

> **Objective**
>
> **SD9.7B** – Know the importance of bees and pollinators for plant reproduction and how they can be endangered by pesticides and human behaviour.

We will learn:

- why bees and other pollinators are important
- about the main threats facing bees and other pollinators
- how these threats can be reduced.

Key vocabulary

agrochemicals, biodiversity, habitats, neonicotinoids, parasites, plant reproduction, pollinators

i We depend for much of our food on bees and other pollinators to ensure **plant reproduction** takes place. Many of our farmed crops are flowering plants and, without pollination by insects, they will not grow.

Pollinators, though, are under threat from human activity and natural causes. These threats include the use of agrochemicals, parasites, diseases, loss of biodiversity and loss of habitat. People are so concerned that some farming practices have been banned in many countries. Also, scientists are researching exactly what is happening and what might be done to ensure these important insects are protected.

Connecting with nature: Session 2

Insects do not consider our need for crops when they pollinate plants. Neither do they consider the plant's need for pollination. So, why do bees and other **pollinators** do this? How does the plant benefit?

1 Select the correct words to complete the text below that describes the relationship between plants and bees.

| nectar | pollen | food | fertilises |

| petals | wax | honey | hive |

When a bee visits a flowering plant, it is attracted by the plant's _____.
The plant produces a sugary substance called _____, which is valued as _____ by the bee and is usually found deep inside the flower.
In order to reach this, the bee brushes against a powdery yellow substance called _____. This is also a valuable source of food for the bee, but it is also the male sperm cells of the plant. These cells coat the hairs on the bee and are transferred from one plant to another. This transfer _____ the plant and new seeds are produced.

The pollen and nectar are taken back to the _____ where they are turned into _____ for food and _____ to make honeycombs for storing the food. In this way, the plant helps the bee and the bee helps the plant.

2 While most flowering plants are pollinated by insects, others are pollinated by, for example, the wind. Rearrange the letters below to spell plants that are pollinated by insects.

yerbrwsrta		esedoli pera	
bcbaega		raugs tbee	
otatmo		rcaufwlolie	

Estimates vary, but pollination by bees and other insects is responsible for about one third of our food crops. If they did not provide this vital service, some common foods would become scarce or not available at all.

Honeybees are under particular threat from human and natural sources.

3 Draw lines to match the description of the threat with the example.

| Use of pesticides to remove insects that would attack the crop | The Varroa parasitic mite carries viruses that infect bees causing disease, for example, deformed wings. |

| Use of herbicides to remove weeds and other competing plants | Removal of trees and hedgerows turns small fields into larger fields, making use of machinery easier but also removing valuable bee **habitats**. |

| Parasitic infestation causing disease | **Neonicotinoids** are used to coat seeds or spray plants to kill aphids or grubs in the soil. The pesticide is toxic to bees and is taken in through the pollen and nectar of treated plants. |

| Removal of trees and hedgerows to make field management easier | Weedkillers are used to clear fields of nuisance plants before crop planting. This reduces the **biodiversity** that bees prefer. |

Connecting with nature: Session 2

The use of **agrochemicals** (herbicides, fertilisers, fungicides and pesticides) and their effect on bees and other pollinators is one of the issues regarding farming and the environment. One solution is to ban the use of agrochemicals.

4 Look at the arguments below and decide what course of action you would recommend regarding the use of agrochemicals. Use the space below to outline your proposals, giving reasons for your decisions. Include other viewpoints if you think they would be useful.

> I manufacture agrochemicals. A ban would put thousands of people out of work.

> Without agrochemicals I would lose over half my crop. How are you going to feed people on half the amount of food?

> Most of the agrochemicals are used to protect crops used for animal food. If we eat less meat, we won't need so many chemicals.

> Bees are insects, put on earth to serve humans. We shouldn't be too concerned about them.

> As a scientist, I can produce genetically modified crops that don't need nearly as many chemicals. But you won't let us use them.

> We should use traditional methods without chemicals and farm organically. The bees are safe and so is everything else.

> If using chemicals means I get my food cheaper, then that's what's important. I'm struggling more than the bees to feed my family!

_____
_____
_____
_____
_____
_____
_____
_____

There is a growing movement to farm organically using traditional methods, without the use of artificial agrochemicals. While this is aimed at a wide range of farming methods, consider what you could do to encourage bees and other insect pollinators. Think about your school and what could be done to increase the honeybee population either through introducing hives or making the habitat more bee-friendly. The following information may help.

Honeybees like:

- plenty of flowering plants, including trees and long grass
- native or wild plants rather than cultivated plants
- plants that flower at different times of the year to give a continuous food supply
- a reliable supply of water
- a hive to live in or at least one that is nearby – less than a kilometre or so away
- shelter from the wind and rain.

Honeybees do not like:

- being disturbed by people or animals
- chemically treated water
- any use of chemical sprays used on plants or to clean paths or buildings
- short, mown grass.

5 Using the information on the page opposite and your own research, draw and label a plan for a part of your school grounds with the aim of encouraging bees. Your labels should explain the choices you made for your plan to be successful.

One crop that is very dependent on honeybees for successful pollination is the almond crop of the USA. The almond trees grow in California but there are not enough native bees to pollinate all the trees. Instead, billions of bees are transported in special hives across the USA. After pollinating the almond trees, they are transported to other parts of the USA to pollinate other crops. Their journeys are as follows:

Arizona to California – almonds

California to Washington State – cherries and apples

Washington State to South Dakota – sunflowers and clover

South Dakota to Florida – clementines and tangerines

Florida to Arizona – winter hibernation

6 Locate the states listed above on the outline map. Draw straight lines between the approximate centres of each state to represent the bees' journeys. Use the map scale to estimate how far the bees are transported during a pollination season. Then answer the questions.

1 Approximately how far do the bees travel during the pollination season? _____

2 Why might this seasonal movement cause harm and suffering to the bees?
_____
_____
_____

3 What **two** alternative solutions might there be to transporting the bees across the USA?

1 _____
_____

2 _____
_____

Connecting with nature: Session 2   85

In this session, you have seen that insect pollinators, and honeybees in particular, are essential if certain flowering plants are to survive. Honeybees face severe threats that include human beings and the way we farm. The use of chemicals, particularly neonicotinoids, and habitat destruction have added to attacks by **parasites** to create a crisis.

There are solutions that require us to change the way we farm. Individually, we can also provide habitats that are bee-friendly. If we do not help the bees, then not only will we lose crops, but we will have shown our inability to live without destroying other species.

7 Explain in your own words the role of bees and other pollinators in the fertilisation of plants.

_____
_____
_____
_____
_____
_____
_____
_____
_____
_____
_____
_____
_____
_____
_____

What new things have you learned?
What had you not thought about before?

Biodiversity and habitat loss (Greater Depth)

Objective

SD9.7C – Know that the illegal wildlife trade is responsible for endangering and causing the extinction of some species and how humankind is trying to combat this.

We will learn:

- what is traded and why
- about the impact of the illegal wildlife trade
- about the people and organisations involved in combating this.

Key vocabulary

biodiversity, biomes, habitat, TRAFFIC, United Nations Office on Drugs and Crime (UNODC), wildlife

Wildlife includes all living organisms that exist without being introduced by people. Wild plants, fish, insects, mammals and fungi are all examples of wildlife.

The illegal trade in wildlife has brought some species to the brink of extinction and threatens many others. This illegal trade can be very profitable. It often depends on global links run by criminal gangs, but is sometimes sanctioned by governments. Criminal trading in wildlife can be obvious (for example, poachers killing a rhinoceros for its ivory); sometimes it is not so obvious.

Ways to combat this illegal trade have become more sophisticated, and international agencies often work together to protect species and break up poaching, smuggling and dealer networks. Disrupting this trade not only helps the wildlife concerned but has wider benefits on **biodiversity** and habitats.

Biodiversity and habitat loss: Session 3

Not all trade in wildlife is illegal. Trade takes place for a wide variety of good reasons. One organisation that monitors both legal and criminal wildlife trade is called **TRAFFIC**. They define the **legitimate** trade in wildlife as:

'Sustainable, legal, fair and transparent. Trade based on sound science and which meets regulatory or sustainability requirements.'

1 Write what you think would be a good definition of the **criminal** trade in wildlife. Think about the words used above. What does 'fair' mean? Why is the fact that it is 'sustainable' important? Why is it regulated?

_____
_____
_____

2 Select the correct words to complete the text below on the nature of legal and illegal wildlife trading.

| sustainable | endangered | pets | animals | plants | valuable |
| overexploited | medicines | food | extinct | species | increases |

Thousands of species of wild _____ and _____ are harvested or caught as part of the legal trade in wildlife. We depend on these species for _____, _____ and _____. As long as this trade is _____ then the species will continue to thrive. When a species becomes _____, it may become _____. If the trade continues, it may even become _____.

The answer is to protect the _____ by making trade in it illegal. However, once this happens, it becomes scarce and even more _____. Criminal trafficking in that species _____ and the species declines even faster.

Biodiversity and habitat loss: Session 3

3 Animal and plant species are illegally traded (or trafficked) for a variety of reasons. Draw lines to match the threatened species with the most frequent reason for why they are trafficked. Most are common, but you may need to look some up.

Species	Reason
rhinoceros horn	luxury rugs
pangolin meat	considered medically useful
rosewood	pets
parrots	jewellery
tiger skins	furniture and wood carving
red coral	food delicacy (mammal)
osprey	ornamental plant
Lady's Slipper orchid	egg collectors
prickly pear cactus	food delicacy (fish)
bluefin tuna	plant collector

Biodiversity and habitat loss: Session 3

Illegal trading in **wildlife** covers a range of criminal activity and attracts well-organised gangs since, in some cases, the profits are greater than the illegal trade in drugs.

Below are the six main types of criminal activity, as recognised by the **United Nations Office on Drugs and Crime (UNODC)**, and a diagram showing a typical chain of supply that criminal gangs organise to conduct this illegal trade.

4 Choose which type of crime fits in the supply chain and write it in the relevant box. Alongside each box is a definition of each type of crime to help you choose.

| Trafficking, dealing, transporting | Importing or exporting | Felling or harvesting |

| Buying, possession, consumption | Processing | Poaching (hunting) |

Type of crime — **Description of crime**

[ ] Unlawful killing or trapping of animals

↓

[ ] Unlawful felling of trees and the taking of plants

↓

[ ] Manufacturing or processing of products that have been taken illegally from plants or animals

↓

[ ] Selling, supplying, storing or transporting wildlife products obtained illegally

↓

[ ] International trade in illegal wildlife products

↓

[ ] Obtaining, owning or using illegal wildlife products

Biodiversity and habitat loss: Session 3

Attempts to combat the illegal trade in wildlife can only be successful if all the motives and viewpoints are understood. Financial gain is only one motive.

5 Imagine you are head of a wildlife protection organisation giving a presentation on 'Why wildlife is trafficked'. Look at the six viewpoints below and then complete the presentation slide by outlining what you think is the **motive** behind each statement.

Think about greed, status, protection, power and influence, for example. Think most of all about what each person or organisation gains from the supply chain. If you explore the three basic operations of obtaining, trafficking and using, you will gain an insight into the motives!

> I poach animals and plants because we are poor and this gives us an income.

> I poach animals because they trample our crops.

> I sell animal products because I can earn more doing this than any other job.

> My customers need wildlife products for medicine or status.

> Drugs, wildlife products, arms – we supply what people want, as long as there is profit!

> I buy wildlife products because they make me feel better.

Why wildlife is trafficked

- _____
- _____
- _____
- _____
- _____
- _____

6 Why does it matter if an animal or plant species is illegally traded to the point of extinction? Rank the statements below from 1 to 10 to show how far you agree with them: 1 for the statement you most agree with; 10 for the one you least agree with.

Statement	Rank 1–10
We have a duty to preserve all wildlife.	
If one species becomes extinct, then many more species that depend on it are threatened.	
The real criminals are the customers who fuel this trade.	
It's illegal. That's the main point. It should be stopped just because it is illegal.	
If we stop the illegal trade in wildlife, then we hit the criminal gangs hard and that stops all sorts of related criminal activity.	
We need to find ways that the people involved can find a better way of making a living so they don't have to take wildlife.	
We can control this trade for the benefit of other species. We could licence plant collection or big-game shooting and use that income to protect others.	
As soon as you make it illegal, it becomes all the more desirable. Remove regulations and illegal trade will disappear.	
It's not important. There are more urgent global concerns other than a few species that no one really cares about.	
There are some species that are really important – dolphins, but not spiders. Spiders are gross! We should protect animals that we like.	

When looking at the illegal trade in wildlife, people tend to focus on a specific animal and the threat to that animal as their numbers decline. Often overlooked is that animal's place within its **habitat**, and the wider consequences if the animal no longer occupies its place in the ecosystem. One example of this is the pangolin. Look at these facts about the pangolin and its habitat:

- The pangolin eats termites.
- Termites are often regarded as pests.
- A pangolin will eat up to 20,000 termites a day.
- According to some research, termites are responsible for 11 per cent of greenhouse gas emissions.
- Termite damage costs the USA over US $1.6 billion per year.
- Some African crops can lose 50 to 100 per cent of their yield due to termite infestation.
- Since 2013, the Cameroonian government has confiscated 8 tonnes of illegally trafficked pangolin scales, representing approximately 25,000 pangolins.
- The pangolin is one of the most trafficked animals, for their scales, other body parts and meat.

7 Imagine you provide online content for a respected news organisation and have to create an article titled: '**It's not just about the pangolins**!'

On the opposite page, write a concise, informative article based on the facts above that describes some of the wider consequences of the declining pangolin population. You could add to the list of facts above by searching online for 'termite damage'.

Think about including an illustration of some kind.

It's not just about the pangolins!

Biodiversity and habitat loss: Session 3

> We have a clear idea about who, why and how the illegal trade in wildlife is carried out, and also that it's not just about a particular species but also about the wider impacts on the environment. So, what can be done to end, or at least disrupt, this trade? Here are some strategies that could be used:
>
> - **Follow the money**. There are huge profits to be made from the illegal trade in wildlife products. Individuals, criminal gangs and even some governments seek to profit from this trade.
>
> - **Target the end user**. There is only a supply of illegal wildlife products because people want them. Stop them and the supply ends.
>
> - **Target the beginning of the supply chain**. If the people poaching or collecting have a better source of income, they will not resort to illegal methods.
>
> - **Appeal to the common good**. If enough people say this is wrong, maybe those involved will realise this, too.
>
> - **Involve governments and agencies** to coordinate a global strategy to end the trade.

8 Research some of the organisations that seek to end the illegal trade in wildlife products. These should include the **World Wide Fund for Nature (WWF)**, the **United Nations Office on Drugs and Crime (UNODC)** and the **Convention on International Trade in Endangered Species (CITES)**.

Now complete the sentences below by adding the correct abbreviated name (from the three listed above) for the organisation that is being described.

_____ : supports states to more effectively prevent, identify, investigate and prosecute wildlife and forest crime.

_____ : works to conserve and protect endangered species, and to address global threats to these, such as climate change.

_____ : an international agreement between governments to ensure that the international trade in species of wild animals and plants does not threaten their survival.

9 Using the information and research from Activity 8, outline your strategy to combat the illegal trade in wildlife, giving reasons for your decisions.

Think about:

- the end users (consumers), criminal gangs and governments involved
- how individuals and organisations can provide a global response to a global problem
- individual species (for example, the pangolin) and also global **biomes** (tropical rainforests, for example)
- the supply chain and how you might intervene at each stage (for example, one person smuggling cacti was stopped at an airport by dogs specially trained to detect plants).

> In this session, you have explored what, how and why wildlife products are illegally traded and trafficked, and the wider ecological effects of this. You have investigated steps that could be taken to end this.
>
> You have learned that while there is a market for this illegal trade, there are profits to be made. The involvement of criminal gangs has made this trade a global concern as it has become part of wider criminal activities that exploit people and the environment.

10 Design a poster to show the harm caused by the trade in wildlife.

What new things have you learned?

What had you not thought about before?

Climate change

Sustainable Development

Objective

SD9.7D – Understand some of the serious impacts of the climate crisis such as extreme weather; floods; droughts and wildfires; water shortages; food insecurity; degradation of soils and migration of populations.

We will learn:

- about the direct and indirect impacts of climate change
- how these impacts are caused by climate change
- who is most affected by the impacts of climate change
- what can be done to mitigate these impacts.

Key vocabulary

bug-out bag, climate change, extreme climate event, food insecurity, hurricane, storm surge, tropical storm, wildfire

---

Climate change is real, and the impacts will severely affect us all, either directly or indirectly. There are those that would question this statement, but scientific evidence overwhelmingly shows that the world faces a global challenge that is of our own making. This challenge has to be addressed through concerted action on the part of individuals, organisations and governments. Such action must tackle the causes of climate change and also the impacts.

In this session, we are mainly concerned with understanding the impacts of climate change. Some of these will cause everyone to reconsider their lifestyles and question things they take for granted. While the impacts of climate change events affect everyone, they affect some people more than others. As is often the case, those who have the least resources to deal with these impacts are those most affected. There are global inequalities that arise out of climate change that, unless addressed, will affect us all.

Climate change: Session 4

Not all natural events are directly linked to **climate change**; some clearly are, some are indirectly linked and some have no link.

1 In the table below, show what link each of the natural events has to climate change by writing either 'Direct', 'Indirect' or 'None' alongside each event type. Most of the events are quite common, but you may need to look up one or two.

Event type	Link to climate change (Direct, Indirect or None)
Tsunami	
Ice cap melting	
Glaciers retreating	
Earthquake	
Sea level rising	
Drought	
Hurricane	
River flooding	
Wildfires	
Volcanic eruptions	

Climate change: Session 4 — 99

Extreme climate-related events have particular properties. For example, hurricanes are characterised by strong winds, heavy rainfall and a tidal surge. These properties will each have their related impacts, some of which may be similar. For example, heavy rainfall and a tidal surge may both cause flooding. These impacts will affect people and the environment.

2 Listed below are the common properties associated with two **extreme climate events**. Complete the table by describing the impacts of these properties on people and the environment. The first one has been done for you.

In the blank row, add another extreme climate event, its properties and its impacts.

Extreme climate event and its properties	Impacts
Hurricane 1. Strong winds 2. Heavy rainfall 3. Tidal surge	1. debris thrown through the air, causing injury and damage to property; power lines falling, which may start fires and cause power cuts; trees uprooted, causing damage to habitats
Heatwave 1. Low/no rainfall 2. High temperatures	

Climate change: Session 4

Extreme climate-related events do not affect all people, regions or countries equally. A similar intensity of **tropical storm** can have very different effects depending on where in the world it occurs. For example, the facts below show the wide variation in impact of two similarly intense tropical storms.

Hurricane Harvey
- Texas (USA)
- August 2017
- Highest windspeed 215 km/h (130 mph)
- **Storm surge** 3.6 m (12 ft)
- 107 deaths
- US $125 billion damage
- _____
- _____
- _____

Bob01
- Chittagong (Bangladesh)
- April 1991
- Highest windspeed 235 km/h (145 mph)
- Storm surge 4.5 m (15 ft)
- 138,866 deaths
- US $1.7 billion damage
- _____
- _____
- _____

3 Research these two events, and add some more facts in each of the boxes above.

4 Explain why there are such differences in the scale of impact between nations in the Global North and those in the Global South.

_____
_____
_____
_____
_____
_____
_____

Climate change: Session 4

Some impacts of climate events are less noticeable but have profound effects. One such example is prolonged low rainfall, or drought. In the USA, this is having a significant impact on agriculture and natural habitats.

5 Choose the correct words to complete this text about the impact of drought.

| dry | Kansas | cooler | drought | 300 | sorghum |
| warmer | Canada | wheat | thirsty | species | hot |

Crop production in the USA is changing as climate belts are moving northwards. Traditional corn-growing areas like _____ are finding it is too _____ and _____. Instead, less _____, more _____ resistant crops like _____ and _____ are being grown.

Further north in _____ – where once only wheat was grown because of _____ temperatures – corn, soybeans and peas can now be grown as the weather becomes warmer.

Farmers can, at quite some expense, change the crops they grow to suit the climate. However, many natural plant _____ cannot adapt quickly enough. Colder habitats are being lost as temperatures increase, while _____ habitats in the south are being destroyed as temperatures become too hot. One of the main problems is that it can take up to _____ years or more for soil – a major component of natural habitats – to adapt to changing climatic conditions.

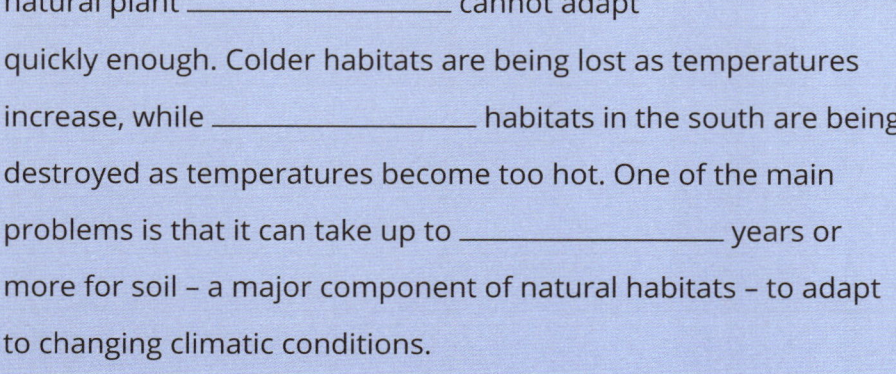

Climate change: Session 4

> Some farmers in the Global North are having to adapt rapidly to climate change challenges and are looking to grow alternative profitable crops. But what about those in the Global South who do not grow crops for profit but to feed their families? What do they do? As the crops they grew for food no longer yield as much, they do not have enough food to sustain them. This is called **'food insecurity'**. They can stay and face hunger, plant new crops that will sustain them, or move. What can be done to help them transition? Is this solely their problem or is it a global problem?

6. Imagine you are part of a United Nations team addressing the issue of how to help farmers in the Global South to combat climate change. Select a problem and outline a strategy that includes **local, national** and **international** solutions. Use these three headings to outline your solution. You may need to research your answers.

Consider specific problems, for example: extreme climatic events (such as tropical storms), sea level changes, crop yields decreasing, increasing pests (such as locusts), wildfires caused by drought. Choose **one** particular event to focus on. What would you advise?

> Here is an example:
>
> Problem = drought
>
> Local solution = teach those affected what new crops they can plant to replace those they used to grow, that will still provide a viable food source.
>
> National solution = provide grants to buy seeds to replace crops with drought-resistant alternatives and training on how to manage them.
>
> International solution = encourage countries in the Global North to reduce carbon emissions and fund programmes to find replacement crops. Provide food aid during the transition.

Problem: _____

Local solution: _____

_____

_____

National solution: _____

_____

_____

International solution: _____

_____

_____

7 There are different solutions for the many impacts of extreme climate change events.

For each of the paired statements, tick the one that you believe offers the better solution for the named impact. Explain your choice. If you think both solutions are equally good or bad, explain why.

Impact: Tidal surge from tropical storm

Solution 1: Build sea defences to protect from tidal surge ☐

Solution 2: Use planning controls to prevent building near threatened areas ☐

Reason: _____

_____

Impact: Drought

Solution 1: Dig deeper wells to access water to irrigate crops ☐

Solution 2: Plant drought-resistant crops ☐

Reason: _____

_____

Impact: Wildfires

Solution 1: Build firebreaks around residential property ☐

Solution 2: Carry out 'controlled burn' of vegetation in threatened areas ☐

Reason: _____

_____

Impact: Ice storms

Solution 1: Provide generators for when power fails ☐

Solution 2: Bury power cables in the ground ☐

Reason: _____

_____

Impact: Tornadoes

Solution 1: Provide smartphone app to track tornadoes ☐

Solution 2: Provide grants to build tornado shelters ☐

Reason: _____

_____

8 Many countries are feeling the impact of climate change through no fault of their own. Imagine you are a community leader of an island. Greenhouse emissions by industrialised nations have caused global impacts that affect your own island community, primarily through a rising sea level and more frequent and violent storms.

Your community lives as an Indigenous nation might: there is little use of modern carbon-based technology on your island. As their spokesperson, you are going to address the United Nations to argue your case for industrialised nations to provide solutions for the problems you feel they have caused.

Write a short speech that states your case and outlines what you expect industrialised nations to do to protect your way of life.

Climate change: Session 4

Apart from what governments and organisations can do to meet the challenges of extreme climate change events, how can we respond on a personal level? You may live in an area directly affected by these events. You may not be directly affected but you might be concerned about them.

For people living in areas directly affected by these events, a survival plan is essential, and that includes what is sometimes called a '**bug-out bag**'. A bug-out bag is a rucksack that contains supplies to help you cope with an emergency. You might have to leave your home with very little notice, in the dark and with no power – because of a fast-approaching **wildfire**, for example.

9 List **ten** items you would include in your personal bug-out bag, and explain why.

1 _____

2 _____

3 _____

4 _____

5 _____

6 _____

7 _____

8 _____

9 _____

10 _____

10 You might be directly affected by an extreme climate event and have need of a bug-out bag. Alternatively, you might be concerned about climate change more generally.

Research ways in which you can personally have an effect on the impacts of climate change. Consider, for example:

- Are there organisations you could support?
- Are there individual lifestyle changes you could adopt to reduce your carbon footprint?
- Are there future career choices you could make to combat climate change?

Think of **six** ways you could make a difference and add these to the diagram.

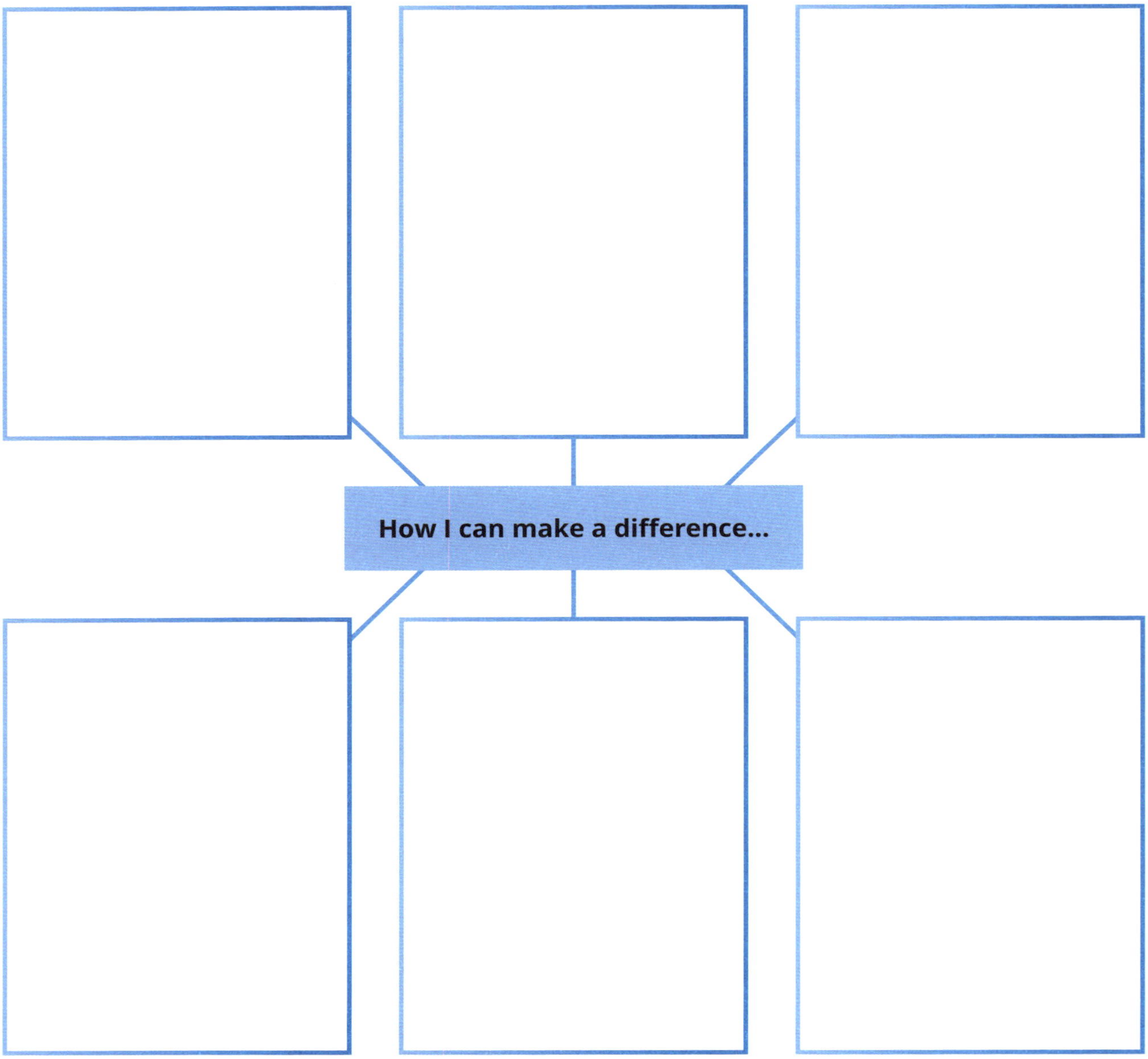

How I can make a difference...

In this session, you have seen that extreme events caused by climate change can have severe impacts that reveal global disparities. Nations in the Global North will suffer material damage, while in the Global South, the loss of life is likely to be far higher. You have also learned that climate change events are not always dramatic. They can happen slowly, but with serious consequences that again reveal inequalities across the globe.

You have considered what can be done at a local, national, international and a personal level to reduce or mitigate these impacts.

Climate change is a real and serious problem that is affecting all peoples across the world. Everyone needs to make a difference if we are to minimise the impact. If we do not, then within a generation or two, the world will be a very different place.

11 Explain why climate change is not only an environmental issue but also a social justice and rights issue.

_____
_____
_____
_____
_____
_____
_____
_____
_____
_____
_____
_____
_____

What new things have you learned?
What had you not thought about before?

Energy, pollution, waste and recycling

> **Objective**
>
> **SD9.7E** – Explore the personal and policy changes necessary to achieve a more sustainable transport system.

> **We will learn:**
>
> - what transport systems are and why they are needed
> - what challenges are presented by transport systems
> - how these challenges can be addressed by sustainable solutions.

> **Key vocabulary**
>
> carbon credits, mode of transport, net zero carbon emissions, transport system

i At any given time, there are about 90,000 cargo ships transporting 5 to 6 million shipping containers across the oceans. On average, there are 9,000 passenger and cargo planes in the sky at any particular moment. In 2020, over 500 million road vehicles were registered in China and the USA. In 2018, India and Japan transported over 17 billion passengers by train.

The global transport system is huge! The need to transport goods and people has led to a growth in transport systems, with some modes of transport – roads, for example – growing faster than others. With this growing need for transport, associated problems have arisen. Congestion, pollution, burning fossil fuels for fuel – all present serious challenges, both for people and the environment.

In this session, you will explore the growth in transport systems and the problems that brings. You will also consider what can be done to achieve more sustainable transport systems and what this means for you, commercial organisations, and both national governments and international organisations.

Energy, pollution, waste and recycling: Session 5 — 109

Transport systems exist on land, sea and in the air. Most result from, and are managed by, a combination of government departments and commercial organisations. Some countries, though, have wholly state-owned systems, particularly rail.

1 Read the report below, written by a student at a school in Conwy, North Wales, United Kingdom. It describes the transport system in the local area. Then answer the questions.

'My school is about half a mile outside the small town of Conwy, which lies on the River Conwy on the North Wales coast.

There is a river taxi, mainly to take people out to boats moored on the river. The A55 is the main road, linking the towns of North Wales. It goes under the river, through a large tunnel at Conwy. It doesn't go through Conwy town but there are junctions to it either side of the town. The main passenger airport is Liverpool John Lennon Airport, over an hour away. Arriva run the local buses, Avanti West Coast run the trains and Transport For Wales is the government department that looks after all transport, including main roads.

I think the problem is that there are very few buses going inland to the villages up the Conwy valley, and often roads are flooded when the river floods or we have heavy rain. There are often accidents on the A55 and on the smaller roads leading up the valley. A lot of the roads are narrow, since there are mainly small villages, isolated farms and cottages once you get outside Conwy. During the summer, tourism increases in Conwy and the car/coach parks and roads get quite congested.

The smaller roads into Conwy and the railway cross the river by bridges. Pollution from these have caused the river to become silted up, making flooding even more common.'

1 List the different 'modes' of public transport mentioned. (A 'mode' of transport means type – for example, car, bus.)
_____

2 Why does the A55 avoid going through the town?
_____
_____

3 What is an advantage of the main airport being over an hour away?
_____
_____

4 Several problems are mentioned. What would be your priority and what should be done?
_____
_____
_____

2 You are going to write a short report about transport in your local area or region. The first step is to research your local or regional transport network and answer the questions below. Use bullet points or notes.

1 How far from your school is the nearest train station, airport and sea or river port?

   _____
   _____
   _____

2 How many major highways are within 20 miles (32 km) of your school? What areas do they link?

   _____
   _____
   _____

3 What modes of public transport are provided within 10 miles (16 km) of your school? (Include, for example, bus, taxi, rail, tram, train, ferry.)

   _____
   _____
   _____
   _____

4 Within your local area, are there any problems with transport? If there are, describe some of them (for example, pollution, congestion, lack of transport). If there are no problems, explain why this is so.

   _____
   _____
   _____
   _____
   _____
   _____

3 Now you have collected some basic information about your local or regional transport network, turn your ideas into a short report. Use the Conwy report in Activity 1 to guide you, particularly in relation to how to structure your writing and how much detail to include.

Energy, pollution, waste and recycling: Session 5

Global transport systems provide the same functions as local **transport systems**: they allow for the movement of goods and people. However, they differ in a number of ways. Most significantly, one key characteristic of global transport systems is the way in which they connect.

4 Choose the correct words to complete the text about global transport systems.

connect	hub	mode
international	dimensions	environmentally
public	ship	interconnected
flights	road	million

Global transport systems are often _____. Air travel, for example, may mean taking local or regional _____ to _____ with _____ flights at a major airport or _____. Most airports are located outside cities and are often connected by _____ transport services.

Large steel containers are used to carry goods by train, truck or _____. All containers are of the same standard _____ so they can be moved easily from one _____ of transport to another.

The most interconnected global transport system is the _____ network. It connects railway and bus stations, airports, and ferry and shipping ports. Businesses, homes and factories are all connected. One estimate is that there are roughly 65 _____ miles of road across the globe, which demonstrates that road transport is the most popular form of transport. It is also why road transport is the most _____ damaging.

Energy, pollution, waste and recycling: Session 5 — 113

Transport systems, while essential, are the cause of two major environmental problems. These are health issues from air pollution and climate change from greenhouse gases. Both of these are produced through burning fuel. Ships, aircraft, cars, trucks and trains all have the capability, either directly or indirectly, to produce emissions that are harmful to people or planet Earth.

5 Emissions from fuel combustion are not the only problems associated with transport systems. Draw lines linking the road transport problem with its matching description.

Congestion	Carbon dioxide exhaust emissions
Poor air quality causing health problems	Too many vehicles using a road
Climate change	Accidents and collisions
Habitat destruction	Street lights to improve safety
Loss of life or injury	Fine particulates in exhaust emissions
Power stations producing greenhouse gases	Tyre and engine sounds
Urban sprawl	Building new roads
Noise pollution	Power generation to charge electric cars
Light pollution	More roads extending towns and cities

6 Research and record in the table below **five** other problems associated with transport. You should:

- name the problem
- name the type or **mode of transport** causing the problem
- provide a brief description of the problem.

Types of transport could include trains, ships or aircraft. Some problems or descriptions may be similar to those listed in Activity 5 in relation to road transport, but look for different ones that are particularly associated with the specific mode of transport.

Transport problem	Mode of transport	Description

Having explored some of the problems associated with transport systems, you will now begin to look at solutions.

Look at the solutions below that countries, cities and major organisations have put in place to combat some of the problems and to develop more sustainable transport systems. The table shows what the solution is, where or who has introduced it and the reason for it.

7 Research **three** other transport solutions around the world and add the details in the blank rows.

Solution	Who/where	Reason
Replace trams with 'Trolza' electric buses	Moscow (Russia)	Improve public transport and reduce emissions
Ban older cars and trucks from city centre	Barcelona (Spain)	Reduce pollution from older, less efficient engines
Liquid petroleum gas for ship engines	Various shipping companies	Cheaper and less polluting than marine diesel oil
Quieter, fuel-efficient aircraft engines	Various aircraft manufacturers	Cut costs and reduce emissions and noise pollution
New 'TGV' high-speed trains and routes	SNCF (state-owned French railways)	Fast rail alternative to roads and national air routes, reducing emissions and congestion
Integrated Cycling Plan	Zhangjiakou (China)	Reduce problems from other forms of road traffic

8 For this activity, you should 'think outside the box'. This means let your imagination come up with solutions that may not even exist using our present technology. Certainly, some solutions for the future are possible because of the speed at which technology is evolving. A zero-emission engine is a good example. Research other examples.

The scenario: Imagine you have been asked to research a transport issue. You have complete control over your regional or global transport systems (road, rail, air and sea). Your one aim is to provide a more **sustainable** solution to the issue while making sure that goods and people can still move freely.

The issue: It could be a single issue (for example, public transit, road transport) or an issue that involves all transport systems within a specific region (including your own) or a global issue.

Give some thought to what you think 'sustainable' means: Do you want everyone to walk or cycle? Do you want **net zero carbon emissions**? Will you offset carbon emissions by buying **carbon credits** from nations in the Global South?

Methodology: Research and develop your sustainable solution. One way of tackling this is to develop principles that should be followed. This is similar to governments putting commitments into law. For example, the United Kingdom (UK) government has passed a law that says after 2030 no new car will be sold that depends on fossil fuel.

Your task: Make notes from your research in the box below. Then on the page opposite, write a report that outlines your plan for a regional or global solution to providing a sustainable transport system for the future.

Use this page to write your report outlining your regional or global transport plan. Make sure that your report includes:

- the regional or global transport issue of concern
- your aims in tackling this issue
- your ideas for solutions – no matter how futuristic!

9 Having outlined a plan for a sustainable regional or global transport system, we also need to consider what can be done at a personal level to make a difference.

Below is a list of personal actions that could contribute to a more sustainable transport system. Choose the **one** that you are most enthusiastic about and in the box below design a poster to promote this action.

- Walk or cycle everywhere when possible.
- Buy a car that doesn't run on petrol or diesel.
- Work for companies that are committed to reducing carbon emissions.
- Use public transport to travel long distances.
- Holiday at home rather than flying to another country.
- Buy locally sourced products.
- Get involved in local, national and global initiatives to find sustainable transport solutions.

Energy, pollution, waste and recycling: Session 5

In this session, you have explored the need for well-integrated transport systems, the problems that can arise from these systems and some of the solutions to such problems, using examples from around the world. You have also looked at how you could personally contribute to sustainable transport.

There is little doubt that developing sustainable transport systems that still meet the needs of a global economy is key to successfully combating climate change and urban pollution. In practice, this means replacing fuel technologies based on oil with less polluting alternatives. At the moment, such technologies are in their infancy.

10 Write the script for a 20-second TV advertisement that outlines a convincing argument for a sustainable transport system. Think in terms of short, snappy points, written as bullet points. If you know of a suitable background music track, then add a note about this!

- _____
- _____
- _____
- _____
- _____
- _____
- _____
- _____
- _____
- _____
- _____
- _____
- _____
- _____

What new things have you learned?
What had you not thought about before?

Sustainable Development

The future of our planet

> **Objective**
>
> **SD9.7F** – Ability to envision an optimistic future for the planet alongside being prepared to act in a way that will achieve it.

> **We will learn:**
> - what it means to imagine a 'healthy' planet
> - about the challenges to achieving a healthy planet
> - how a healthy planet could be achieved
> - about the need to set clear goals and targets.

> **Key vocabulary**
>
> analyse, SMART targets, Sustainable Development Goals (SDGs), synthesise

i Planet Earth is beset with problems and challenges – for example, global inequalities, rights abuses, climate change and pandemics. It would be easy to think that there is nothing that can be done. The truth is that the people on planet Earth have always faced challenges that have called for governments, organisations and individuals to find solutions. The challenges we presently face can also be overcome.

It is a big task to develop a plan to ensure a healthy future for our planet. The skills you will need to develop are the ability to '**analyse**' and '**synthesise**' your learning – that is, to break down what you have learned (analyse) and put it back together as a coherent plan (synthesise). As you progress through the activities in this session, you will be asked to think about and analyse what you have learned and then to create or synthesise your plan for a healthy planet using your skills and knowledge.

The future of our planet: Session 6

What is meant by a 'healthy planet'? It is important that you consider at the beginning what you want your plan to achieve.

Aldous Huxley wrote a famous book called *Brave New World*. In it, the 'World State' is a global government that runs the entire world. Its motto is: 'Community, Identity, Stability'. In this novel, a healthy planet is seen as one that is controlled, and where people live as one global community; where personal identity is determined at birth; and where people lead stable, happy lives.

1 Complete the sentence below describing what you would consider to be the definition of a 'healthy planet'. Then think of a motto and write it in the space provided.

A healthy planet is…
_____
_____
_____

My motto for a healthy planet is…
_____
_____

2 In the box provided, design a 'healthy planet' logo that reflects the message in your motto.

3 Look at the table below. It lists some of the issues facing planet Earth that you have explored during your Global Citizenship course.

For each issue, describe the problem and give at least one example. The first row has been completed for you. Then, in the blank row at the bottom of the table, try and add another issue that you think is particularly concerning. Finally, in the 'Priority' column, indicate which **three** issues would be your top priorities to address. Write 1, 2 and 3 against your priority issues, with 1 being your highest priority.

Issue	Description of the problem	Example(s)	Priority
Climate change	Unsustainable use of fossil fuels has created greenhouse gases that are heating the atmosphere and changing our climate.	Polar ice caps melting Extremes of weather	
Poverty			
Rights abuses			
Sustainable transport			
Equality and discrimination			
Environmental impacts			
Justice, law and order			
Food, water and energy			

The future of our planet: Session 6   123

The United Nations has identified 17 **Sustainable Development Goals (SDGs)**. These goals represent issues of global concern that the nations of the world must tackle together to ensure we have a healthy planet. Each goal has specific targets. They include examples of **SMART targets**. SMART means:

S = Specific – so the action is focused on meeting the target

M = Measurable – so progress can be seen and you know when the target has been reached

A = Attainable or Achievable – so the target is realistic and not beyond reach

R = Related – so the effort is linked to your values or those of the organisation

T = Time-limited – so action is taken and not delayed

4 Research the SDGs. Do any of them match your top three priorities from Activity 3? Can you spot SMART targets being used?

Now write a SMART target for each of your first three priorities from Activity 3.

SMART target for Priority 1:
_____
_____

SMART target for Priority 2:
_____
_____

SMART target for Priority 3:
_____
_____

The future of our planet: Session 6

The COVID-19 pandemic that started in 2019 is a good indicator of how global economies and lifestyles can be affected when drastic change is needed to combat a global threat. The text below describes one change that resulted from the pandemic, together with the reasons and consequences. It also describes the knock-on effects that resulted from that change and what these could mean for the prospects of achieving a healthy planet.

Change
There was a shift from office working to working from home. This was partly a choice by organisations and partly due to government restrictions on travel. On average, 50 per cent of office workers across European cities worked from home at some point during the pandemic.

Reason for change
COVID-19 is easily transmitted when people spend any length of time close to one another. By working from home, close contact could be avoided and transmission of the virus reduced.

Consequences of change
People didn't have to commute to their offices, so there was a drastic reduction in road, rail and other commuter traffic. In Rome in Italy, for example, rail and metro traffic dropped as low as 5 per cent of normal values, especially during the various lockdowns.

In London in the UK, many coffee shops, fast food outlets and retailers found that the drop in commuter numbers severely affected their businesses. Some reported up to a 90 per cent drop in earnings, while many lost 50 per cent of earnings. On the other hand, one food delivery company, Pale Green Dot, went from supplying 100 per cent of their orders to businesses to supplying 95 per cent of orders to households. Within a few days, they had to move to larger premises and employ extra people to keep up with demand.

Lessons for a healthy planet

Positive
- Reducing transport reduces pollution and greenhouse gas emissions.
- Buying locally sourced food instead of imported food cuts transport pollution, improves food security and encourages local food producers.

Negative
- Many shops and other retailers depend on office workers to keep their businesses open.
- Fewer people are needed to run public transport services, increasing unemployment among these workers.

5 Choose another change brought on by the pandemic, either from the ones opposite or one of your own. Research the change, using the same format as the example above to explore it: Change, Reason for change, Consequences of change, Positive and negative lessons. Try to include specific examples, with facts and figures, as in the example.

Present your research on the page opposite.

The future of our planet: Session 6 — 125

| Closure of schools and rise of online schooling | Increased status of health workers in society | Rapid development of vaccines and medical equipment | Rise in online sales to replace 'walk-in' customers | Restrictions on all public gatherings, including sports |

The future of our planet: Session 6

To reach the goal of a healthy planet, changes are needed, and a plan to achieve the targets has to be made and followed.

One key concern is whether the global economy is incompatible with, for example, reaching climate change targets or many other sustainability targets needed to ensure a healthy planet. Countries, organisations and individuals value growth: it is one of the main ways of measuring success. Businesses want to make bigger profits each year; people want to see their salary increase every year. In order for this to happen, factories need to produce more, shops need to sell more and people need to buy more.

Some people argue that some of the SDGs are themselves unsustainable given the need for economic growth. This is one reason why achieving a healthy planet is not easy. Saying, for example, 'Get rid of petrol and diesel engines' or 'Provide secondary education for every person' may be difficult to achieve in an economy geared towards growth.

6 Select the correct words to complete the text about economic growth.

| strong | limited | unsustainable | weakening | power stations | value |
| lithium | ethical | equilibrium | factories | iron ore | GDP |

One measure of the success of an economy is _____ (Gross Domestic Product). This is the _____ of all the goods and services of a country. When GDP increases, a nation is seen as having a _____ economy. If it decreases, this is a sign of a _____ economy.

Some people argue that continuous growth is _____. For example, building new _____ and _____ uses resources that are _____; there is only so much _____ or _____ (to make batteries for cars that can replace petrol engines).

So, for a healthy planet, some argue that we need the economy to be more _____. Also needed is a replacement for GDP as a measure of success; instead of valuing growth, economic systems should value _____, or balance. Measuring well-being, food, water and energy security, for example, is seen by some as more sustainable and more important than how much money the world makes.

Before developing a plan, or as part of one, there needs to be some consideration of how any necessary changes are going to be made. You have seen that there may need to be some shift in the way the global economy is viewed, but what about governance? (You will remember that governance means the way in which a central body – a national government, for example – organises public institutions to create policies, pass laws and make decisions.) Would there need to be any changes in the way the world is governed?

7 There are many systems of government. Draw lines to match the type of government to its description. Some you will know; others you may have to look up.

Type	Description
totalitarian	Elections take place and voters choose people or political parties to represent them
monarchy	One-party state that governs centrally the whole country
anarchy	A single person rules for life, usually by birthright
unitary	There is no formal government; the country is ruled by local leaders
democracy	Absolute control over the population, agriculture and industry

The types of government listed above are just examples and highlight an important issue when planning change: how will the plan be carried out?

8 Describe how you would organise the governance of your plan. That is, what kind of organisation would be needed to make sure the plan is carried out?

_____
_____
_____
_____

9 On the opposite page, you are going to create your plan for ensuring a healthy planet.

There are some requirements for the plan:

1. It should have a short statement defining what you mean by a 'healthy planet', followed by a motto (see Activity 1).

2. It should identify three issues or goals, each with a short summary of the challenge (see Activity 3).

3. For each issue or goal, there should be at least one SMART target (see Activity 4).

4. For each issue, there should be a brief explanation of the expected positive consequences of carrying out the plan (see Activity 5).

5. It should include a short statement outlining changes in the economy that might, or might not, be needed for the plan to succeed (see Activity 6).

6. It should include a short statement describing what type of governance will be needed to carry out the plan (see Activity 8).

You can use the work you have produced for all the previous activities. However, look at them again and make changes to improve your ideas.

The future of our planet: Session 6 | 129

Charter for a healthy planet

In this session, you have given some thought to what it means to have a healthy planet and the factors that need to be considered in achieving this goal.

You have seen that if things stay as they are, then there will be obstacles to achieving a healthy planet, but that these obstacles could be overcome providing people, countries and organisations have clear goals and targets. Economic and political systems may also need to change to support what needs to be done.

Achieving a healthy planet is a complex task but there are enough people who believe it is important for it to be SMART!

10 Describe what a healthy planet would look like to you. What are the **three** most important things people need to do to help achieve your vision?

_____
_____
_____
_____
_____
_____
_____
_____
_____
_____
_____
_____
_____
_____

What new things have you learned?
What had you not thought about before?

Who am I?

Identity and Diversity — 131

> **Objective**
>
> **ID9.2A** – Understand that identity can be complex and a positive sense of self is crucial.

We will learn:

- what is meant by 'identity'
- what is meant by a 'sense of self'
- why a positive sense of self is important.

Key vocabulary

attributes, behaviours, identity, self-esteem, sense of self

ⓘ A person's identity is likely to be shaped both by behaviours (what people do) and attributes (things that are physically or naturally theirs, such as eye colour and bone structure).

A newborn baby will have unique attributes but, usually, few unique behaviours. As that child grows and develops, a set of behaviours develops. These may be learned from parents, siblings or friends. They may be ways the child conforms to the expectations and demands of society. They may reflect the opportunities the child has. They may link closely to their attributes.

As people develop further, they may consciously alter their behaviours or attributes in order to influence their identities. For example, someone may choose to develop an identity as an athlete by training hard, or dye their hair a different colour.

Developing a sense of self – understanding your identity – is often vital for good **self-esteem**. Generally, people with a well-developed sense of self can make more independent choices. People lacking a sense of self may struggle to understand what it is they want out of life, relationships or their careers. They may make choices based on what other people think, rather than their own wants and needs.

132 Who am I?: Session 1

1 Select the correct words to complete the text about the concept of identity.

| influenced | aware | cultural | decisions |

| **sense of self** | **attributes** | family | happy |

People's identities can be made up of both _____ and **behaviours**. As people grow and experience more, their behaviour will be _____ in different ways. Such influences may include _____, friends and society; they may be _____. This means that people have the potential to change their behaviour throughout their lives.

Knowing who you are (that is, understanding your identity) is called your _____. Generally, a well-developed sense of self means people are more _____ of their responses and behaviours. They are more likely to make their own _____ rather than doing only what others say they should do. They also become more able to understand what will make them feel _____.

2 Add to the diagram to show some of ways in which you think your behaviour is influenced.

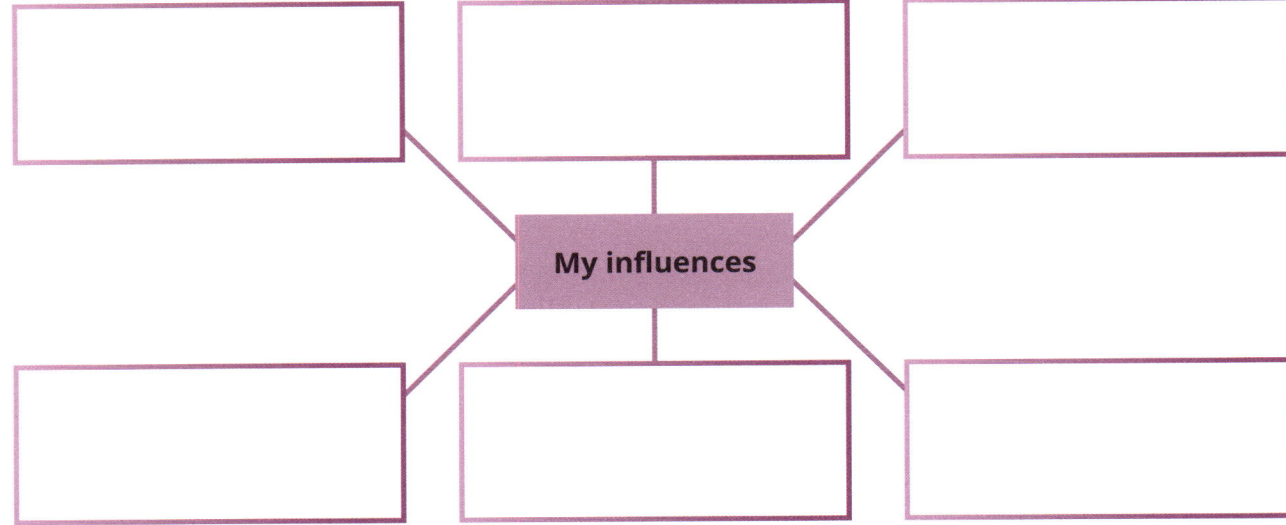

By your age, you will already have developed views regarding your **identity** and the identity of others. These views are unique to you, but may also reflect social and cultural norms or expectations – sometimes called 'stereotypes'.

Everyone expresses their identity in a very personal way. This could be through the clothes they wear, the way they stand, the interests they have, the people they like or the social groups they join. Some people are very aware of how they express their identities and make deliberate choices. Others are less aware, and express themselves naturally without making deliberate choices.

3 Answer the questions below to explore to what extent your choices are deliberate.

1 What affects your choice of clothing?
___
___

2 How do you choose which people to count as your friends?
___
___

3 If you feel awkward with a group of people, what do you do?
___
___

4 How do you choose your leisure activities?
___
___

5 How do you make important decisions?
___
___

Who am I?: Session 1

A 'sense of self' comes from understanding who you are and why you are like that. The following statements are indicators that a person might have a less well-developed or negative sense of self.

1. Finding happiness in only other people's happiness or success
2. Having difficulty separating your thoughts and feelings from the thoughts and feelings of people close to you
3. Having difficulty creating and maintaining boundaries regarding how you are treated, and how you treat others
4. Displaying poor time management
5. Losing your sense of self in relationships by trying to copy others
6. Feeling lost or without a direction in your life
7. Having difficulty setting goals and making decisions
8. Believing what your social group believes or pressures you to believe
9. Feeling overwhelmed by other people, as if they are somehow better than you
10. Feeling suspicious or doubtful of yourself, your values and your decisions
11. Feeling that other people are taking advantage of you
12. Feeling empty

4 Write the opposite of each of the statements above. For example, for the first one you might write 'Finding happiness in your own achievements'.

Try to decide whether your own sense of self is reflected in the list above or the list you have written.

1. _____
2. _____
3. _____
4. _____
5. _____
6. _____
7. _____
8. _____
9. _____
10. _____
11. _____
12. _____

5 Listed below are some of the things people can do to improve their sense of self. Think about each suggestion and write notes on the lines below it.

1. Think about what things make you happy. List the things you like and appreciate, such as films, books, foods, clothes and music.

   - _____   - _____
   - _____   - _____
   - _____   - _____

2. Think about what you value. List some of the areas in life and causes you care about. For example, spending time with your family or campaigning against climate change.

   - _____
   - _____
   - _____

3. Act on your values. List a few ways in which your actions reflect your values and beliefs. This could be a choice of hobby or the way you act around people.

   - _____
   - _____
   - _____

4. Develop your own interests. List a few new activities you would like to explore, whether or not you think your friends will enjoy them too. You might be surprised by who will be interested, or who you may meet.

   - _____   - _____
   - _____   - _____

5. Share your feelings. What situations make you happy or proud? Note down **one** of them. Do you experience situations that make you tense, anxious or sad? Note down **one** of these, too. In both cases, sharing your feelings can help you and others feel valued. Note down some ways you could share your feelings about each situation.

   _____
   _____
   _____
   _____
   _____
   _____
   _____

Who am I?: Session 1

6 The first column in the table below lists a number of situations. Fill in the other columns using words or short phrases to describe behaviours that could be shown by someone with a positive sense of self, and someone with a more negative sense of self.

Some answers have been completed for you as examples.

Situation	Positive sense of self	Negative sense of self
Outlook on life	Feeling positive and confident with a sense of direction	
Time management		
Likes and dislikes		
Relationships		
Saying 'no'		Finding it difficult
Making decisions		
Values and beliefs		
Self-awareness		
Personal care	Having a healthy diet and doing exercise	
Interests and activities		Joining in only when asked

7 Imagine you have a friend who asks you for some advice. Read what your friend says and then write some notes below, showing how you would respond.

Consider your response carefully, in the light of what you have learned about identity and self of sense. Will you offer solutions to the problems or will you consider the wider issues?

"I don't know what to do. I'm fed up. I'm behind in my work and my teachers are getting annoyed. I keep having arguments at home about what I'm going to do with my life. I don't know what I'm going to do next week, never mind the rest of my life!

I'm getting teased by my friends because either I don't dress like them or, when I do, I'm called a copycat. I don't much like them, anyway. I feel uncomfortable with them. They don't usually ask me to meet up with them – but when they do, and if I don't, they go on about why I didn't.

I sit at home staring at the walls of my room. I don't know what to do."

_____
_____
_____
_____
_____
_____
_____
_____
_____
_____
_____
_____
_____
_____

Who am I?: Session 1

We all have an 'identity', and it is your choice how you express that identity. Developing a positive sense of self is recognised as a major influence on our well-being. Of course, people with a good sense of self are not always positive, forward-looking and able to excel in any situation. Similarly, people with a less-developed sense of self are not all withdrawn, uncertain and unable to see a way forward. However, improving your sense of self may help you achieve what you want from life.

There are many online resources, ranging from quizzes to professional advice, that can give you more information on identity and sense of self. Your school or local library will have a range of resources and contacts you could consider. Your school will also have people you can talk to if you have concerns.

8 Write an eight-line poem that explains what identity means to you. Turn a question you may still have about identity into the last line of your poem.

What new things have you learned?
What had you not thought about before?

Identity and Diversity | 139

Humankind: all equal; all different

Objective

ID9.2B – Ability to use research skills to critically evaluate stories in the media about people who are trying to gain equality for who they are.

We will learn:

- what is meant by research skills
- that what we read or watch is not always true
- how to check the reliability and validity of a story
- how some people have fought to achieve equality.

Key vocabulary

equality, evaluate, fact checking, fake news, news organisations, reliability, research, reverse search, social media, validity

> Inequality exists in many different forms across the world. Combatting this to achieve equality is the goal of many organisations, such as the United Nations. Sometimes, individuals play an important part in this through sharing their own personal stories about how they tried to gain equality. These stories are told by the people involved, news organisations and social media. Some of these stories are true and some are false. Some are based on fact, some on opinion.

Humankind: all equal; all different: Session 2

News items, online articles and **social media** posts should be trustworthy. They should be both valid and reliable. These are two important concepts when researching.

- **Validity** is concerned with accuracy.
- **Reliability** is concerned with consistency.

Look at the following statements concerning a watch:

- My watch is five minutes fast.
- My watch is always five minutes fast.
- My watch is reliable but not valid.
- My watch is consistently inaccurate.

In other words, because my watch is five minutes fast, it is not accurate (it is not valid). However, because my watch is *always* five minutes fast, it is consistent — consistently fast (it is reliable). Moving the minute hand back five minutes would make the watch reliable and valid!

The concepts of reliability and validity (consistency and accuracy) apply just as much to the stories we watch and read as to the watch.

1 During the 2008 Presidential campaign in the USA, many news organisations ran stories that became known as the 'Birther Movement'. This campaign sought to prove that Barack Obama could not become President because he wasn't born in the USA.

Research this story and check it for reliability and validity, using the search term 'Birther Movement'. Then answer the following questions.

1. Are the claims that Barack Obama was not born a United States citizen valid? How do you know?
   _____
   _____

2. Are the claims that Barack Obama was not born a United States citizen reliable? How do you know?
   _____
   _____

3. Why do you think these claims were made?
   _____
   _____

4. Who made these claims?
   _____
   _____

5. Do these claims represent an **equality** or a discrimination issue? Why?
   _____
   _____

Activity 1 highlighted a number of factors to be taken into account whenever you are researching stories. These include:

- Who is writing the story? What is their motivation?
- Are the facts correct? How will you check them?
- Is the story based on fact or opinion?
- Is there another story that offers an alternative opinion?

There are online resources that will help you to check stories. Search for '**fact checking**' to access some of these tips. There are also many games and quizzes that test how well you can spot what is trustworthy.

2 Imagine you are writing an online article for your school magazine on fact checking. You are reviewing what you consider to be the three most informative and fun activities available. Look for well-respected **news organisations** for your examples and include:

- a factsheet
- a game
- a link to a fact-checking tool

Use the space and headings below to outline your review.

Factsheet

Source: _____

Brief description: _____
_____

Your opinion: _____
_____

Game

Source: _____

Brief description: _____
_____

Your opinion: _____
_____

Fact-checking tool

Source: _____

Brief description: _____
_____

Your opinion: _____
_____

3 Where do you find the information for your research? How do you know those sources are trustworthy?

Look at the list below showing some of the commonly used sources. In each box, write a number between 1 and 5 that reflects how trustworthy you think that source is. Trustworthy can mean whether you think it is true or whether a person actually said what is reported. 1 = very trustworthy; 5 = very untrustworthy.

- [ ] Wikipedia
- [ ] Government website
- [ ] Websites of known organisations
- [ ] Websites of unknown organisations
- [ ] Printed books
- [ ] Online books
- [ ] Online news organisation
- [ ] TV news media
- [ ] Magazines
- [ ] Professional journals

- [ ] Social media posts from friends
- [ ] Unknown social media posts
- [ ] Direct quotes from people
- [ ] An individual's blog
- [ ] Newspapers
- [ ] An unnamed 'source'
- [ ] An interview with a named person
- [ ] A scientist
- [ ] A journalist
- [ ] A politician

4 Explain how you decided which sources are more trustworthy than others.

_____
_____
_____
_____
_____

Humankind: all equal; all different: Session 2   143

Here are a few tips to help you ensure that your research is based on trustworthy sources.

- Always find more than one source to check your information.
- Always try to find direct quotes from the people concerned.
- Look for the 'hidden agenda'. What is the real reason for the story being written?
- Use tools to check sources. Fact-checking websites will cover most major stories but not all. **Reverse search** images to check their origin.
- Check the language used. Is it straightforward, factual reporting leaving you to form an opinion? Or is it using emotive language to try and get you to believe the writer's opinion?
- Make sure you are using the story to help you form, not support, an opinion.
- Look for balance in a story. Are both sides of an argument presented?
- Search online for advice from reputable sources by using the search terms 'checking the truth of a story', 'fact checking a story' or 'how to spot **fake news**'.

5 Choose **one** of the two stories about the COVID-19 pandemic below. Using the tips above, research the two opposing viewpoints for the story, and then answer the questions that follow.

Story 1 – Vaccinating against COVID-19	**Story 2 – The origins of COVID-19**
Viewpoint 1 – vaccinations are safe and will protect people	Viewpoint 1 – COVID-19 was manufactured and deliberately released
Viewpoint 2 – vaccinations are unsafe and cause harm	Viewpoint 2 – COVID-19 originated in an animal and mutated to infect people

1 What source(s) did you use to check viewpoint 1?
_____
_____

2 What source(s) did you use to check viewpoint 2?
_____
_____

3 Which viewpoint do you think is more valid and reliable? Give reasons for your answer.
_____
_____
_____

Humankind: all equal; all different: Session 2

6 Imagine you are a fact checker for a large, respected news organisation. Your task is to research stories and use your research skills to **evaluate** them. When evaluating the story, remember you need to consider the following.

- What is the aim of the story? Is it factual reporting or is it trying to get you to believe something?
- Is the story based on someone's opinion or on facts?
- Is the opinion balanced or one-sided?
- Are the facts correct?
- Are images used correctly?
- How is language used? Is the language neutral or emotional?
- Can you detect any bias in the story? If so, what?
- What sources are referred to? Are they valid and reliable?
- Do you trust the story? Do you think it is true?

You have been asked by your editor to find online stories or articles for a special feature on people who have had to overcome obstacles in order to be treated equally. The editor has said you can pick your own stories if you wish but has provided the notes below suggesting three people. Your editor has also said (in **bold**) what type of story is needed and included other instructions.

Read your editor's comments. Then use the opposite page to provide links to your chosen online stories/articles, plus your notes giving reasons for these choices.

Kathrine Switzer: First woman to run in an official marathon – Boston marathon. Race number 261 – good photo of an official trying to pull her out of the race – 'women can't run' – 'running causes damage to internal organs'. She formed running clubs for women – introduced women's marathon to Olympics. **Need a story that is unbiased reporting of her. Must include why she wanted to run and why others didn't. Angle = equality for women.**

Nelson Mandela: South African – arrested and imprisoned for treason – was freed and fought for equality of the Black population of South Africa – controversial figure – viewed by some as a terrorist and by others as a hero. **Need two angles: one shows him as respected leader, freedom fighter; other shows him as a danger and threat. Angle = rights.**

Emmanuel Ofosu Yeboah: Paralympic athlete from Ghana – tough childhood because of disability. 'Disability doesn't mean inability' – check 'ABLE' magazine or 'Emmanuel's Gift' (documentary about him). **Need a story showing how he overcame disability prejudice. Must be factually correct. Angle = disability equality.**

In exploring how important it is to research and assess how trustworthy a story is, you have looked at:

- what is meant by reliability and validity
- what research sources are more trustworthy
- how to assess stories for particular purposes.

Remember: all social media stories, mainstream news stories, books, magazines and TV programmes want you to believe what you are reading or watching. It is important that you ask the right questions before forming your own opinions.

Equally important is that you have good research skills so that you can check stories quickly. Practise using the online tools and fact-checking websites. Pay careful attention to the language used. Soon you will be able to spot the fake from the genuine article.

7 Explain why it is important to critically evaluate stories in the media.

_____
_____
_____
_____
_____
_____
_____
_____
_____
_____

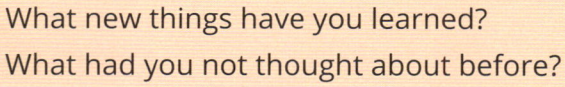

What new things have you learned?
What had you not thought about before?

Challenging prejudice and discrimination

> **Objective**
>
> **ID9.2C** – Ability to recognise the unquestioned wisdom, truths and normality of a dominant group, and actively challenge it when it causes prejudice and discrimination.

We will learn:

- about the difference between prejudice and discrimination
- how to recognise prejudice and discrimination
- about protected characteristics
- about different types of discrimination
- how prejudice and discrimination can be challenged.

Key vocabulary

direct discrimination, discrimination, harassment, indirect discrimination, prejudice, protected characteristics, victimisation

Prejudice can mean several things but, here, it means that someone has an unfair or unreasonable opinion about another person or group of people that is formed without thought and usually without direct experience.

Discrimination means that people are treated differently, and usually worse, than other people because of a real or imagined difference.

Essentially, prejudice is what we think and discrimination is what we do.

In this session, you will explore why people become prejudiced and how that can lead to discrimination. You will also examine how prejudice and discrimination can be opposed by governments, organisations and you personally.

1 If **prejudice** is concerned with what we think about another person or group of people, where do those thoughts come from?

Add to the diagram to show what or who influences how we think about other people.

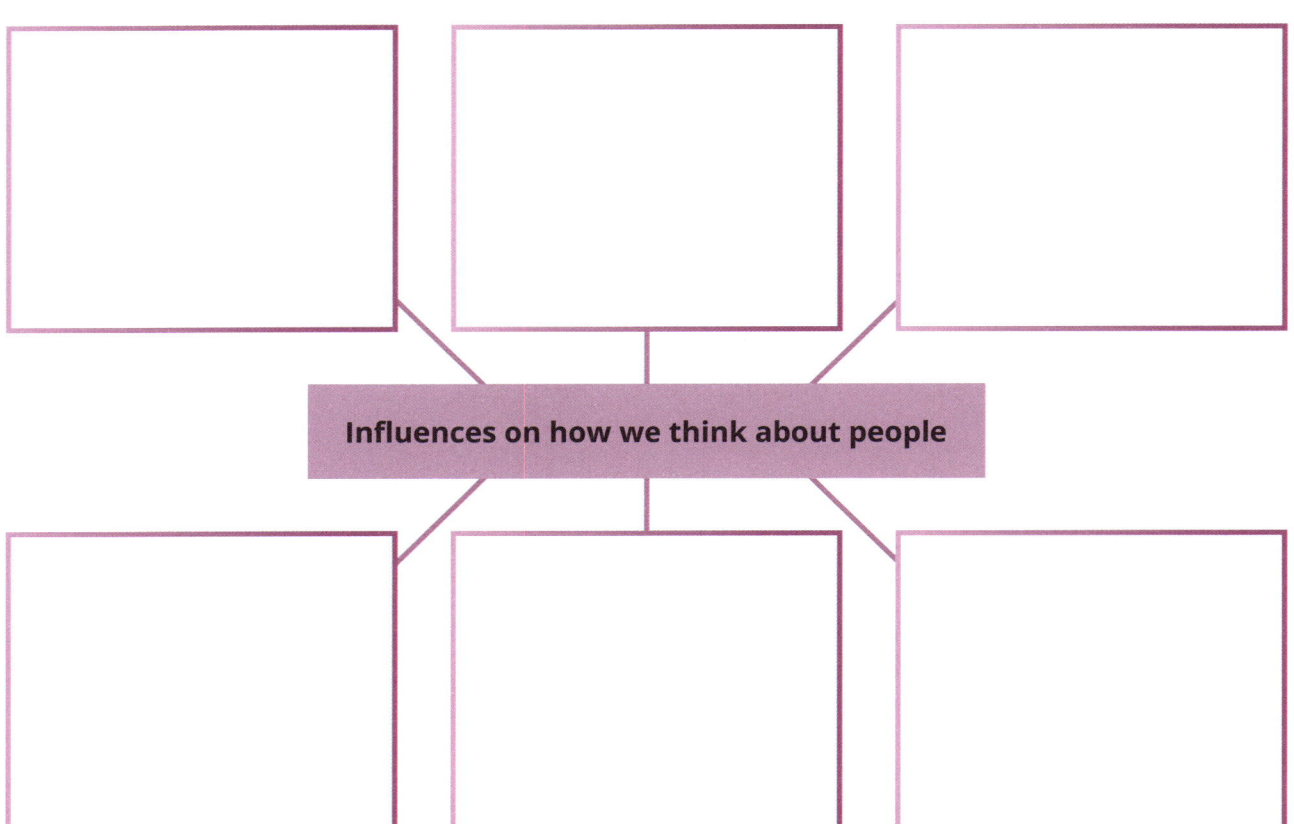

There are many influences on the way we think. Look at the list below and see if you included them in your diagram. If not, add them now.

- **Ignorance**. Often we just don't have the knowledge to make an informed opinion. Sometimes, though, we don't want to gain that knowledge because our prejudice reinforces our feelings of superiority over other people.
- **Social groups**. We sometimes form our opinions from parents or friends. There may also be celebrities we like and listen to.
- **Stereotyping**. The media often promotes stereotyping to create opinions about whole groups of people based on the characteristics or actions of individuals.
- **Scapegoating**. This is when a person or group is blamed for something usually unrelated to them.

Challenging prejudice and discrimination: Session 3

When people's thoughts and opinions lead them to treat other people or groups unfairly, prejudice becomes **discrimination**. There are different types of discrimination. The types listed below have been chosen because, in the UK, they are '**protected characteristics**'. This means it is against the law to discriminate against people on these grounds. Some of these types of discrimination will be familiar to you, others less so.

2 Research the protected characteristics below. Then write a sentence for each to explain how you think discrimination on these grounds is shown. The first one has been done for you.

Age

When people are treated unfairly because they are thought to be too young or old for a certain situation without a valid reason.

Disability

_____
_____
_____

Marriage and civil partnership

_____
_____
_____

Pregnancy and maternity

_____
_____
_____

Ethnicity

_____
_____
_____

Challenging prejudice and discrimination: Session 3

> It is likely that every person has one or more protected characteristics that could lead to them being discriminated against. Protected characteristics explain **what** might be discriminated against. You should also consider **how** that discrimination might take place.
>
> There are four common ways in which people are discriminated against:
>
> - **Direct discrimination**
> - **Indirect discrimination**
> - **Harassment**
> - **Victimisation**

3 Read through the descriptions and examples of discrimination below. In each space, write which type of discrimination, from the four listed above, you think is been described.

_____ : This occurs when someone is discriminated against specifically because of their protected characteristic. For example, a person applying for a job is disregarded because they might become pregnant.

_____ : This happens when people are disadvantaged by a general policy or action. It isn't aimed at a specific protected characteristic but has the same effect. For example, a company expects everyone to be available for weekend working, even though some employees will have strong religious beliefs against such activity.

_____ : This is when people or organisations create a hostile, humiliating or degrading environment. For example, if a person with a disability is refused entry because they might 'upset' other customers.

_____ : This is more specific and occurs when someone raises a concern in relation to discrimination and action is taken against them. For example, a person complains of having to work longer hours than anyone else and then finds they have been sacked for some obscure reason.

Challenging prejudice and discrimination: Session 3 — 151

4 Read the two school-based case studies below. See if you can work out and add the following information: the protected characteristic; the type of discrimination taking place; the prejudice behind the discrimination; the action that should be taken.

Case study 1 – Inaya

Inaya, a Year 9 student, fasts once a year, for a month. When this becomes known, members of her football team upset her by saying it will make her a worse player, and threaten to drop her from the team. She speaks to the head of Year 9, who talks to some of those involved. Now Inaya is having a worse time because she tried to do something about her problem. She feels it would have been better if the teacher hadn't been told.

Protected characteristic	Type of discrimination	What is the prejudice?

What should happen?

Case study 2 – Sami

Most of the time Sami's disability doesn't cause her too many problems that she can't solve. Sami is a talented musician but doesn't get involved in school music because she cannot manage her cello and her wheelchair at the same time, and she gets fed up having to ask people to carry her cello to and from the music rooms. She doesn't take part in school concerts because she has to be lifted on and off the stage and she finds that unpleasant.

Protected characteristic	Type of discrimination	What is the prejudice?

What should happen?

Challenging prejudice and discrimination: Session 3

> It is difficult to take action against prejudice because it means taking action against what people think. This does not mean it should not be challenged, but it is easier to take action against discrimination because something has to happen for discrimination to take place. Most countries have laws that protect their citizens from discrimination, and most organisations and businesses will have policies to ensure they treat people fairly and equally.

5 Describe an experience you or someone you know has had where discrimination took place. As you explain what happened, try to identify three things:

- The protected characteristic that was being discriminated against
- The type of discrimination that took place (direct, indirect, harassment, victimisation)
- The prejudice that you think was behind the discrimination

_____
_____
_____
_____
_____
_____
_____
_____
_____
_____
_____
_____
_____
_____
_____
_____
_____
_____

6 Research case studies of discrimination. Then provide a 'treatment' for a video that explores an example of discrimination at school or in your community. A treatment is a short summary that outlines the plot, the characters and the outcome. It could also include any locations that might be used and 'key' dialogue, scenes or shots.

Include a title at the beginning and, at the end, explain why you think your video should be made.

154 Challenging prejudice and discrimination: Session 3

> In this session, you have explored prejudice and discrimination, and seen how people are protected in law from discrimination. Although prejudice can be difficult to challenge, when it leads to discrimination, it can be challenged effectively.
>
> Even an individual can challenge discrimination. One way to do this is to 'make a pledge' – a commitment or promise to do something either to help change things in general or to challenge a particular discrimination problem.

7 Think about your own school or community. Identify a discrimination issue you could challenge and, working either on your own or with other people, make a pledge to improve the situation. Could you, for example, be a role model or an equality and human rights champion? Set out your pledge below, explaining:

1. what your pledge is
2. what discrimination problem it will help to tackle
3. how you are going to make it happen.

_____
_____
_____
_____
_____
_____
_____
_____
_____
_____
_____
_____

What new things have you learned?
What had you not thought about before?

People and places around the world

Globalisation and Interdependence 155

Objective

GI9.3A – Appreciate that knowledge and skills flow in all directions between communities and countries.

We will learn:

- that the world has a globally interdependent internet network
- that knowledge and skills development depends on global flows
- about the advantages and disadvantages of global interdependence.

Key vocabulary

global connectivity, internet (data) cables, network, telecommunications, World Wide Web

During the early 1800s, the quickest way to get a message from China to the UK was by tea clipper. It took just under a hundred days for these fast cargo ships to cross the 11,000 nautical miles (20,000 km) between the ports of Hong Kong and London. The arrival of the electric telegraph in the late 1800s meant that a message could be sent and a reply received on the same day.

Today, high-speed internet cables mean that the average 'ping' time is just over 200 ms (milliseconds). Ping is the time taken to send a small amount of data from one point to another and back again. From 100 days to 200 ms! The growth in global **telecommunications** technology has been astounding and is a good example of globalisation and interdependence.

The ability to communicate almost instantly clearly has advantages, but what are they? And what are the disadvantages?

1 The map below shows the flow of data through **internet cables** that circle the world. Development of the internet (a network of networks) began in 1983. Since then, over 900,000 km of cable has been laid, much of it along the ocean floor. These cables carry over 95 per cent of internet traffic. Look at the map and answer the questions below.

1 Where are the greatest concentrations of data cables?
   _____
   _____

2 Why are there large areas of land without data cables?
   _____
   _____
   _____

3 Africa seems to have a higher density of mainland data cables compared with North America. Why is this? (Hint: 'Leapfrog technology' allows internet access via mobile phones rather than computers.)
   _____
   _____
   _____

2 Select the correct words to complete the text describing the extensive function of the internet.

data	roads	files	emails
network	global	ARPANET	Defense
Timothy	smartphone	websites	internet

Most of us use the terms **World Wide Web** and the _____ to mean the same thing – but they're actually quite different.

The World Wide Web comprises the pages you see when you're online on a computer or _____ . It was invented by Sir _____ Berners-Lee in 1989 and, in 1994, the public first came to use _____ .

The internet is the network of connected computers that the web works on, and that are also used for sending emails and files. It was developed in the 1960s by the Department of _____ in the USA to allow computers to communicate with each other and was called _____ (Advanced Research Projects Agency NETwork). This is where Berners-Lee used it as a research scientist and recognised its potential for _____ use.

Imagine the internet as the network of _____ connecting towns and cities, and the World Wide Web as the things you see on the road network like houses, shops and bridges. The vehicles are the _____ using the _____ . Some go between shops, factories and homes (websites) and others will be transferring _____ or _____ using the internet, without the need for the World Wide Web.

158 People and places around the world: Session 1

3 It is hard to imagine life without the internet. Below are six ways in which people might use the internet and/or the World Wide Web. In each of the three empty keyboard buttons, add another use that you make of the internet.

Online banking is what I use it for most.	Social media mainly, and messaging and video calls.	I use it mainly for streaming videos and music.
I occasionally send an email. That's about it, really.	I spend a lot of time looking up things – facts, news stories, that sort of thing.	Shopping! Clothes, books, food. All done online.

4 Draw lines to match these internet-related terms with their definitions.

hardware	A program that lets you use the World Wide Web to view internet pages
uniform resource locator (URL)	To copy information from your internet-enabled device to the internet
download	Information stored on computers
browser	A website that lets you search for other websites by typing in words that define the content you are looking for
internet protocol (IP)	Transmission of a file from one computer system to another
operating system (OS)	The machinery, wiring and other physical components of a computer system
search engine	The main program that controls the operation of a computer
data	A unique sequence of numbers and full stops that identifies each computer on a network
upload	The address which links to a specific web page

It would be difficult for any business or organisation with a global reach to function without the internet. However, it is not just large corporations that benefit from **global connectivity**.

BBC Janala is an example of how internet technology can improve education in Bangladesh. Here are some basic facts about this initiative.

- 95 per cent of the adult population of Bangladesh have access to a mobile phone with internet access.
- BBC Janala allows people in Bangladesh to access short audio lessons and SMS (text) messages to improve basic English language skills.
- Lessons include 'Essential English' and 'English for Work'.
- All the six major Bangla mobile networks have agreed to offer connections at the low price of 50 paisa (0.004 GBP) per minute.
- The mobile lessons also link to the programme website, which provides interactive online learning.
- The lessons are also produced in print in the leading Bangla newspaper.
- Over 20 million people access the programme.

5 Research BBC Janala. Use your research, and the basic facts above, to produce an infographic or article for an online magazine, describing the initiative, on the page opposite. Use images or diagrams to illustrate key facts. Use the box below for making notes.

People and places around the world: Session 1 161

The internet and the World Wide Web have become essential in many ways. The world economy depends on them. Utility services, including power and transport, cannot function without them. Development programmes like BBC Jamala need them in order to provide their services. But the internet and World Wide Web are vulnerable. For example:

- The cables that form the internet are reaching their capacity but the amount of data is rapidly increasing.
- The World Wide Web is unfiltered, which means anything can be put online, including criminal and terrorist activity, particularly using readily available 'dark web' tools.
- Cyberspace – the virtual computer world – is becoming a battleground for state-sponsored cyber attacks, all dependent on the internet.
- Vital undersea internet cables can be threatened with disruption or destruction by hostile states.
- The World Wide Web can be used as a means of oppression by states who use it to monitor dissidents and restrict freedoms.

6 Research any **one** of the vulnerabilities listed above (or choose one of your own) and, in the space below, produce a list of facts outlining the situation and explain what you think the consequences might be.

_____
_____
_____
_____
_____
_____
_____
_____
_____
_____
_____

You have seen from the examples in this session that the combination of the internet and the World Wide Web provides us with one of the most complex and useful systems that reflect our global interdependence. Yet it has only been in existence for 25 years or so.

What do you think will happen in the next 25 years? Will 'the internet of things' develop, so that we become a truly interconnected society with, for example, our fridges monitoring their contents and automatically placing orders to replenish their stocks? Or will its vulnerabilities lead to a breakdown in this global network?

7 Outline your vision of what the internet and the World Wide Web will be like in 25 years' time.

> In this session, you have explored how the internet and the World Wide Web can drive our economies and allow countries in the Global South to access skills that bring opportunities and challenge inequality. However, it is important that we ensure that it is used for good, and not malicious, purposes. As Timothy Berners-Lee says in 'Answers for Young People':
>
> "Any really powerful thing can be used for good or evil. Dynamite can be used to build tunnels or to make missiles. Engines can be put in ambulances or tanks. Nuclear power can be used for bombs or for electrical power.
>
> So what is made of the Web is up to us. You, me, and everyone else.
>
> Let's use the web to create neat new exciting things.
>
> Let's use the Web to help people understand each other."

8 Draw a flow chart that gives an example of how the internet helps knowledge and skills flow in all directions around the world, helping us to learn from each other.

What new things have you learned?
What had you not thought about before?

Globalisation and Interdependence 165

Global trade, ethics, production and consumption

> **Objective**
>
> **GI9.3B** – Explore what it means to be an ethical entrepreneur for whom the well-being of people and the planet is a key consideration.

> **We will learn:**
>
> - about different types of economic system and company
> - about market forces
> - whether market forces and ethical entrepreneurship can coexist
> - the principles of ethical entrepreneurship.

> **Key vocabulary**
>
> economic system, ethical entrepreneurship, market forces, private company, public company

> i
>
> An ethical entrepreneur is someone who conducts their business while considering the well-being of people and planet Earth, and is not concerned only with making a profit or self-advancement. Clearly, the business must be successful, otherwise it would cease trading, but is it possible to be both ethical and profitable? There are many who think it is, and in this session, you will look at examples where this is the case.
>
> Before that, it is useful to understand how companies are owned and how the economy functions. These concepts provide the framework within which a successful entrepreneur will need to operate.

An **economic system** describes the way goods, services and capital (money) flow between producers and consumers. There are four basic types of economic system.

Each type of system has its advantages and disadvantages.

Traditional economic system

This system is found in the most traditional and ancient societies. Such societies tend to be rural, with farming or fishing as the main industries. Each person has a role to play, often working in close-knit family groups. The economy generally produces just what is needed to maintain a society's standard of living.

Command economic system

In this type of system, the economy is controlled centrally, usually by the government. The government controls what will be produced, how much it will cost and how much people will be paid. Although individuals may own the companies, the government controls their decisions. The government will usually directly own critical industries, for example, rail, utilities and aviation.

Free-market economic system

In this type of system, government intervention is kept to a minimum. Companies produce what consumers want and charge what their customers are willing to pay. In a free-market economy, companies will seek to maximise their profits, but competition from other companies means products are sold at the lowest cost to satisfy their customers. Government intervention will be challenged. Defence, utilities and transport, for example, are controlled by companies seeking a profit rather than the government providing the services.

Mixed economic system

This combines the command and free-market systems. The government retains some state control over sensitive or critical industries but allows companies to operate and respond to **market forces**. The government will pass laws to regulate the economy, for example, to ensure environmental and employee standards or to prevent a company creating a monopoly (where a company controls the total supply of a product). Some industries – transport, for example – will be state-run.

Global trade, ethics, production and consumption: Session 2

1 Alongside each description in the table below, write whether you think it refers to a 'traditional', 'command', 'free-market' or 'mixed' economic system. Then answer the question below.

Advantages	Economic system
The government can mobilise resources to meet the needs of the populations and provide jobs for everyone.	
Lack of regulation means costs can be driven down to produce the cheapest possible goods and services.	
The economy has developed over the years to be sustainable, using indigenous technologies.	
Although there is some regulation, there is also constant innovation as companies try to be more competitive or to develop new products.	
The government can intervene to ensure workers' rights are maintained and can set minimum pay levels.	
Disadvantages	**Economic system**
There is rarely a surplus or profit.	
There is a lack of innovation since central control removes individual initiative.	
Since the economy is driven by self-interest and profit, disadvantaged groups, particularly the poor, will suffer.	
Those industries that are state-run may need government subsidies since there is no competition to cut costs.	
Production is controlled and may not reflect demand. There may be unwanted surpluses or critical shortages of goods and services.	

Which type of economic system do you think will be most likely to reflect ethical principles? Give reasons for your answer.

_____
_____
_____
_____

Global trade, ethics, production and consumption: Session 2

Companies are owned in a variety of ways. The type of ownership will affect how the company conducts its business and may affect the extent to which it can adopt ethical principles.

2 Select the correct words to complete the text about common types of ownership. Then answer the question below.

company	decisions	collectively	goods	sells	invest
meetings	members	shareholders	owner	advice	profit

Private company: A private company belongs to the owner. The _____ will decide how the company will progress, what its aims are and what _____ or services it _____. The owner may take _____ from people both within and outside the company but will ultimately take the responsibility for all decisions and make the _____.

Public company: A public company will be run by a board of directors with a chief executive officer taking overall responsibility. The _____ issues shares for sale and _____ invest in the company. They _____ in the expectation that they will make a profit on their investment, but the board of directors make the _____. However, special _____ are held where the shareholders can ask the board of directors to justify their decisions.

Cooperative: A cooperative is owned and run by its _____ – the people who use its products and services. Major decisions are usually taken _____ and any profits are returned to the cooperative to develop the business or to be used as the members wish.

Which type of company ownership do you think will be most likely to follow ethical principles? Give reasons for your answer.

_____
_____
_____

Global trade, ethics, production and consumption: Session 2

It is possible for ethical trade and entrepreneurship to operate within any particular company structure and within any one of the global economic systems. But what does ethical trade mean? One organisation promoting ethical trade is the World Fair Trade Organization (WFTO).

The WFTO has produced a set of 10 principles that guides the companies it works with.

3 Research the 10 principles of the WFTO. Choose **three** principles and write a brief explanation of what each one means. An example has been given for you.

Capacity building: a commitment to develop the business skills and abilities of producers

1 _____
_____
_____

2 _____
_____
_____

3 _____
_____
_____

Global trade, ethics, production and consumption: Session 2

4 From the ethical companies listed below, choose **one** from Group A and **one** from Group B. You may not be familiar with all these companies. Research your chosen enterprises and then complete the fact boxes below.

Group A: Costco; Sony; Starbucks; Patagonia; WH Smith; LUSH

Group B: Asha Handicafts Association, India
Classic Alpaca, Peru
Bombolulu Workshops, Kenya
Thanapara Swallows Development Society, Bangladesh
Wild Tracks Kahawa International, Tanzania

Group A

Name of enterprise: _____

Type of company (Private, Public, Cooperative, Other): _____

Economic system (Traditional, Command, Free-Market, Mixed): _____

Description of enterprise: _____
_____

Explain to what extent it is an example of an ethical company.
_____
_____
_____

Group B

Name of enterprise: _____

Type of company (Private, Public, Cooperative, Other): _____

Economic system (Traditional, Command, Free-Market, Mixed): _____

Description of enterprise: _____
_____

Explain to what extent it is an example of an ethical company.
_____
_____
_____

5 Imagine you are an entrepreneur looking for an opportunity to establish a new ethical enterprise. Outline the characteristics of your company, addressing these questions:

- Who would own the company?
- What type of company would it be?
- What economic system would you prefer?
- What would be your guiding principles?
- What type of enterprise would it be?

Give reasons for your decisions. Present your company profile in the form of an infographic or written report in the box below.

Global trade, ethics, production and consumption: Session 2

Whether it is an outerwear chain with a presence in all big cities or a worker's cooperative in a remote part of the world, you have seen that there are opportunities for **ethical entrepreneurship**.

Just as importantly, you have explored the economic conditions and company ownership models that might influence such enterprises, and the guiding principles that could ensure its ethical dimension is embedded.

6 Annotate the outline below with some key principles that an ethical entrepreneur would adopt. One has been done for you.

Fairness

What new things have you learned?
What had you not thought about before?

Global wealth and poverty

Globalisation and Interdependence — 173

Objective

GI9.3C – Interest in and motivation to challenge financial inequality and promote poverty eradication.

We will learn:

- how to take action to challenge poverty
- about tools for decision making
- about creating a resource portfolio.

Key vocabulary

Boston Square, criteria, decision matrix, flow diagram, resource portfolio, scoping

ℹ️ We live in a world where financial inequality is common. Some people are very rich; even more people are very poor. In between are a lot of people who have enough for their basic needs and varying amounts left over. The amount left over after food, shelter, fuel and other basic necessities have been paid for is called disposable income. People living below the poverty line have little or no disposable income.

In this session, you will learn how to take action to draw attention to those living in poverty and suggest ways to help them. As part of this, you will explore how to use specific project management tools to help you in this and other tasks or projects.

1 A **flow diagram** is one simple, yet common technique for showing the stages of a task in their logical sequence. In this case, the task is to take action to challenge poverty.

This task has been broken down into the six stages shown below.

Decide on the correct sequence and write the stages in the boxes of the flow diagram. The first stage should be in the box at the top of the diagram. Alongside the diagram are brief notes concerning each stage.

When you have finished, answer the question below.

| Carry out project | Decide on project | Finish |
| Collect information | Start | Research options |

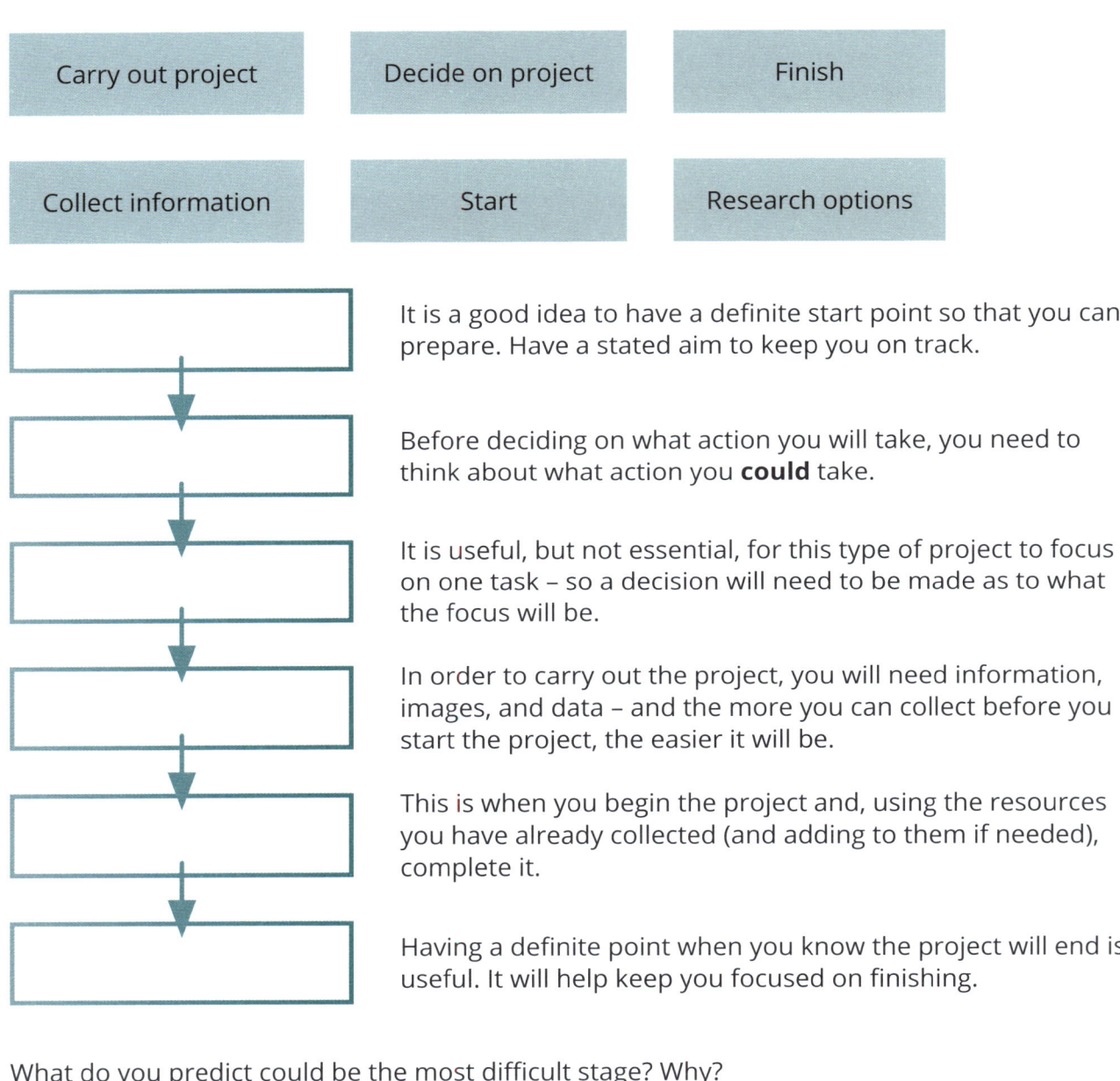

It is a good idea to have a definite start point so that you can prepare. Have a stated aim to keep you on track.

Before deciding on what action you will take, you need to think about what action you **could** take.

It is useful, but not essential, for this type of project to focus on one task – so a decision will need to be made as to what the focus will be.

In order to carry out the project, you will need information, images, and data – and the more you can collect before you start the project, the easier it will be.

This is when you begin the project and, using the resources you have already collected (and adding to them if needed), complete it.

Having a definite point when you know the project will end is useful. It will help keep you focused on finishing.

What do you predict could be the most difficult stage? Why?

_____
_____
_____

Following the flow chart in Activity 1, your stated aim might be, for example:

Carrying out a project to help people in poverty

How are you going to do this? What are your options? There are many things you could do, including:

- Write an article for your school magazine.
- Produce posters to put up around the school.
- Write a letter to your local elected representative.
- Collect donations for a charity working with poverty.
- Organise a school assembly.
- Organise a food collection for a food bank.
- Search on the internet for ideas, using the term 'How can I help poverty?', for example.
- Ask other people what they think might be good.

It is important that you consider more than one option, otherwise you might find you are committed to a project that doesn't work.

2 Research options and record **three** things you could do. You can include one suggestion from the list above but you must research the other two ideas yourself.

1 _____

2 _____

3 _____

At the end of the research stage, there will be several alternative projects you could undertake. One way of deciding which to choose is to use a decision matrix. A decision matrix will have the alternatives you researched and the criteria you will use to help you decide.

The criteria are the factors you think will affect your decision. For this activity, the criteria chosen are:

- **Interest –** How interested are you in the option? The more interested you are, the more successful it will be.

- **Difficulty –** A project that is easy to carry out might be better than one where you have to solve lots of problems to achieve success.

- **Impact –** A project with a high impact is going to have more effect than one with a low impact.

- **Resources –** How easy is it to find what resources you will need? Your initial research will have given some indication if they are readily available – if they aren't, you will struggle to find them.

3 The **decision matrix** for this activity is on the opposite page. It includes the criteria and four of the example options listed on the previous page. Follow these steps:

1. Add one of your own options to the matrix, in the final, blank row.

2. Look at the first criteria (Interest) and, out of all five options, decide which one will be awarded the maximum 5 points (the most interesting one). Then award 4, 3, 2 or 1 point to the other options, in descending order of interest, with 1 point for the least interesting.

3. Do the same for the other three criteria.

4. Total each row.

5. The row with the highest score should be the best option.

If any options result in an equal score, then they are equally suitable.

When you have finished, answer the questions below the table.

Options	Criteria				Total
	Interest (5 = Most interesting)	**Difficulty** (5 = Least difficult)	**Impact** (5 = Biggest impact)	**Resources** (5 = Easiest resources to find)	
Write an article					
Put up posters					
Collect food					
Write a letter					

1 Which option scored highest? _____

2 Which option scored lowest? _____

3 Which options, if any, scored equally? _____

4 How would you decide between options that scored equally? (Hint: The answer lies in the criteria.)

_____

_____

_____

5 To what extent did the highest-scoring option agree with your instinctive feeling about it?

_____

_____

_____

6 To what extent did the lowest-scoring option agree with your instinctive feeling about it?

_____

_____

_____

Once you have chosen your project, you then need to gather the resources to enable you to carry it out. It is much better if you research and gather your resources before you actually start to produce your project. Look at the two statements below. They describe two people.

Kit: Kit starts her project straight away. Fairly soon, she discovers that she needs a new resource to enable her to proceed. As she find new resources, she realises that they are revealing gaps in her project. She ends up with a project driven by each new resource.

Noah: Noah spends time researching resources he thinks link to his project. As he gathers resources, he gets a shape for his project. Once he starts his project, he uses those resources but as it develops, he finds gaps. He looks for resources to fill the gaps.

Building a **resource portfolio** – a system of files to store and organise your resources – helps you shape your project.

Kit has made the classic mistake of starting a project without a shape beforehand. The alternative, as followed by Noah, is to carry out **scoping**. Scoping means to research the project at the beginning to find what is relevant and what is worth including or discarding. Scoping can be defined as 'mapping a project to define key concepts, types and sources of evidence and to identify gaps'.

4 Based on your understanding of scoping, what advice would you give to Kit? Write this in the space below. As part of your answer, explain why scoping is undertaken once the project has been decided rather than when deciding what project to undertake.

_____
_____
_____
_____
_____
_____
_____
_____
_____
_____
_____
_____

Global wealth and poverty: Session 3   179

You have wisely decided to scope the project and gather resources before starting on the project itself. But what resources should you include?

5 Choose the correct words to complete the text below about the types of resource to collect.

| pasting | copyrighted | internet | project | paper | time |
| Images | organised | business | income | folder | guide |

The resource portfolio can take several forms. It could be a box with _____ files. However, it is more likely to be computer-based, since most of your research will use the _____ .

There are several apps that can help you organise your resources, but using folders to organise them will help. Organise your files to suit your _____ . Using a _____ just for images, for example, might be useful. Or you could arrange resources according to the 'sections' that you are using to undertake your project.

_____ , text, weblinks and videos can be included, but it is also useful to create a document that you use to note important concepts or headings to _____ your project.

Remember that you need to use 'copyright free' resources where possible. If you find a resource that is _____ , you may not be able to use it. Many sources allow use of these resources providing it is for non-commercial purposes and you are not a _____ using it to generate _____ . Check this before use or find a copyright-free resource that is similar. Rewrite text and put it into your own words rather than cutting and _____ it.

Above all, make sure your resources are _____ . It is frustrating to waste _____ looking for them because you had no system.

Following the flow diagram you created in Activity 1, you have now started your project to challenge poverty. Even for simple projects, there will be quite a few tasks that have to be completed. One way of keeping track of these is to make a list of them all. The problem is, which to do first? In other words, how do you prioritise the tasks?

One useful management tool to use is a variation of the '**Boston Square**'. This helps you decide on priorities and is shown in the diagram below.

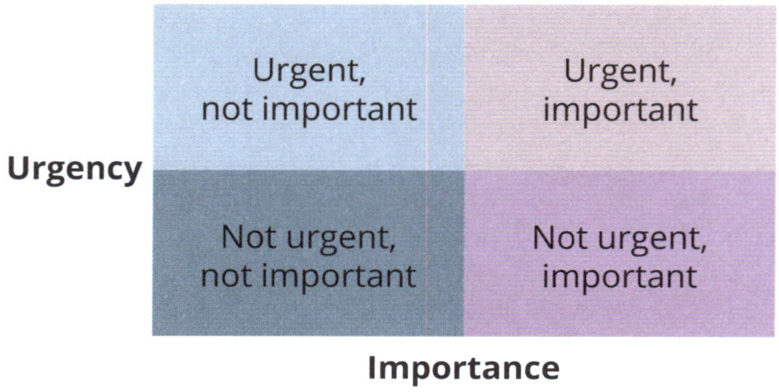

Urgency	Urgent, not important	Urgent, important
	Not urgent, not important	Not urgent, important

Importance

6 In the table below, list **five** personal or school tasks you need to do. Use the diagram above to decide which are 'Urgent, important'. These are your first priority. Your next priority are 'Urgent, not important' tasks, followed by 'Not urgent, important' and, lastly, 'Not urgent, not important' (which might not need doing at all!).

Task	Priority

In this session, you have looked at some basic project management skills and tools that can be used when carrying out a project to challenge poverty.

The flow diagram you created in Activity 1, on which the activities in this session are based, includes two stages that have not been explored: 'Start' and 'Finish'. They are quite important steps but can be addressed with two simple questions:

How do you know when you have started your project?

How do you know when you have finished?

7 Suggest ways that you could challenge financial inequality either globally or within your local community. Present your ideas as a bullet list.

- _____
- _____
- _____
- _____
- _____
- _____
- _____
- _____
- _____
- _____
- _____
- _____
- _____

What new things have you learned?
What had you not thought about before?

Information, technology and communication

Objective

GI9.3D – Knowledge of some of the dangers posed by hackers, trolls and cyberbullies and know ways to combat these abuses.

We will learn:

- how the internet is used for subversive or illegal purposes
- how people can protect themselves from internet-based harm.

Key vocabulary

cyberwarfare, disinformation, misinformation, phishing, ransomware, scamming

Most people would agree that the internet is a complicated place to be, especially for the unwary, ill-prepared or uninformed.

There are many people and organisations, some state-sponsored, that use the internet and the World Wide Web to commit crimes, influence people, spread lies, hurt people and conduct warfare.

In this session, you will explore some of the ways in which cyberspace is unsafe and also some of the ways this is being challenged.

1 Misuse of the internet and the World Wide Web comes in many forms. Draw lines to match the type of misuse to its description.

Type	Description
trolling, flaming	Concerns that legal corporations are trawling personal data for commercial gain
disinformation	Revealing private and personal information about a person or organisation
ransomware, phishing, scamming	Malicious or political attacks that flood computer systems with requests
cyberattack	State monitoring and manipulation of social media to exert control over a population
denial of service/distributed denial of service	Using social media to promote false information or conspiracy theories
doxing	State-sponsored use of cyberspace to disrupt computer systems of other nations
misinformation	Personal attacks against individuals to cause emotional harm or discord
repression	Attacks by individuals or criminal gangs for financial gain
invasion of privacy	Using social media to alter public opinion for political purposes – often state-sponsored

2 As well as what might be called 'traditional' warfare, nation states are increasingly using cyberspace to carry out attacks on other nations. Select the correct words to complete the text describing such attacks.

| location | uranium | critical | state |

| artillery | servers | propaganda | cyber |

State-sponsored _____ attacks are conducted by one nation _____ against another. The purpose of these attacks is to compromise _____ systems, sow dissent, extract information or expose weaknesses in systems.

One example of such an attack targeted the control systems used in the production of nuclear fuel from _____ .

Other examples of state-sponsored cyber attacks might include attempts to compromise national _____ -targeting software or to infiltrate the _____ of foreign parliaments in order to extract sensitive information.

The difficulty with these types of attack is that while the _____ of the attackers can probably be estimated, providing conclusive evidence that a nation state is responsible becomes a _____ war in which one side blames the other. In turn, both deny all knowledge and dismiss the allegations as unjustified speculation.

Misinformation and disinformation may sound the same, but they are quite different. Knowing the difference helps you to understand the purpose or intention behind a story, post or article.

Misinformation is inaccurate information that is originated or shared. The person sharing it is misinformed. They may believe what they are sharing is correct, but they are wrong.

Disinformation is intended to deceive. The person originating or sharing it knows it is false; it is a deliberate attempt to sow discord for political, commercial or ideological gain.

3 Complete the table below by showing whether you think each scenario is an example of misinformation or disinformation. Then answer the question below.

Scenario	Misinformation or disinformation?
A company employs people to post false and damaging reviews about a rival company.	
An individual reads a social media post that promotes false anti-vaccination information and reposts it, thinking it to be true.	
A website for a political party deliberately spreads conspiracy theories about an opposition party knowing them to be untrue.	
A national sports drug-testing organisation only publishes data for athletes from their country who have tested negative for banned substances. They omit those who test positive.	
A politician misreads his speech and instead of saying, 'There is not a crisis', says, 'There is a crisis'. The online headlines report **'CRISIS'**.	

Misinformation and disinformation are concerned with intent. How, from something you read, listen to or watch online, would you tell one from the other?

_____
_____
_____
_____
_____
_____

Individuals and criminal gangs are constantly finding new ways to deceive people in order to commit cybercrime. Their aim is get money or information. One common way they do this is by 'phishing', or its related 'spear phishing'.

Phishing is where you are persuaded to reveal personal information – for example, your username, passwords, bank card details and PINs – that is then used in criminal activity.

The methods vary but often involve receiving an email saying your account has been compromised and asking you to click a link to make your account secure. The link identifies you and gives the criminals the login details to an online bank account or retailer. Now they can login as you, and divert money to their account or order goods to be delivered to their address.

The key to combatting phishing is:

1. recognising a phishing email
2. ensuring that you have strong passwords
3. enabling two-factor authentication.

Spear phishing happens when the email contains personal information – your name, for example. This is to make you think it is more genuine. Criminals trade lists of personal information to make their attacks more effective.

Information, technology and communication: Session 4

4 Having read the information about phishing on the page opposite, now read the speech bubbles. Then answer the questions below.

Target 1
I got an email from my bank saying my account had been hacked and could I verify my details. So I did.

Target 2
The email from an online shopping site had my name, so I thought it was genuine. I went into my account and everything seemed fine.

Target 3
I use a strong password with two-factor authentication. No one will ever ask for this in an email or link. I report any attempts.

Target 4
My username is 'username' and my password is 'Password' (with a capital 'P' to be safe).

Target 5
The email said to click on the link, so I did. I guess I should have opened the web browser as I normally do.

1 Which number target is most likely to be the victim of phishing? Why?
___
___
___

2 Which number target is least likely to be the victim of phishing. Why?
___
___
___

3 What is two-factor authentication and why should it be used? (You may need to research this.)
___
___
___

4 What makes a password 'strong'?
___
___

5 Scamming is where you are invited to send money to a criminal – and many do! It is fraud. There are many types of online fraud. Draw lines to match each type of fraud (centre column) with an example (left-hand column) and advice on avoiding it (right-hand column).

Example	Type of fraud	Advice
You are offered a 'Game Pass' at a low price. It is not available on the official web page.	recruitment fraud	Always use the official site. If there are bargains, this is where they will be.
Designer clothing is offered on a 'Buy Now' auction site at a fraction of the normal price.	romance fraud	Only buy tickets through authorised agents. Otherwise you will be refused entry.
A website offers guaranteed part-time work providing you pay a registration fee.	ticketing fraud	If it's too good to be true, then it isn't true. Avoid bank transfers and use online payment transfers for security. Never send cash!
You become online friends with someone who would like to meet you – if you could help with the air fare.	auction fraud	No reputable employment company would ask for this.
Your friend says there is a website selling ticket 'returns' for your favourite band at low prices.	online selling fraud	If you send money, there will be another request for more.

6 Ransomware is one of the fastest-growing areas of cybercrime. Research the following questions in relation to it.

1. What is ransomware?
2. Who are the most likely targets of ransomware?
3. How does a ransomware attack happen?
4. What are the most effective methods of preventing ransomware?

Using this research, design an informational poster that warns of the dangers of ransomware attacks and advises how to guard against them.

Read each statement below. If you agree with it, place a tick next to it. If you disagree, place a cross. Then answer the questions below.

Statement	✓ ✗
1. Internet use should be monitored for evidence of criminal activity, for example, child abuse images.	
2. If people don't want their personal details used by internet companies, they shouldn't agree to the terms and conditions.	
3. Monitoring of people for criminal activity should only be carried out by a court order.	
4. Governments should be allowed to remove posts that are critical of the way the country is run.	
5. Social media platforms should remove users that promote political, religious or social unrest.	
6. The internet should be completely free from commercial or political intervention. You should be able to post anything.	
7. Social media companies should be held responsible for what is posted on their platforms in the same way that book publishers are.	
8. Governments should not be able to restrict access to the internet.	
9. There needs to be tighter regulation of the internet and what is published – either on social media or on other websites.	
10. People should be able to use the internet without revealing any personal information.	

1 Which number statement do you most strongly agree with? Why?

_____

_____

2 Which number statement do you most strongly disagree with? Why?

_____

_____

Information, technology and communication: Session 4

In this session, you have explored some of the ways in which cyberspace can be used for criminal activity, state-sponsored **cyberwarfare** and spreading falsehoods. You have seen how these take place and some of the methods used to offer protection.

Another area of concern is cyberbullying or online abuse. If you are concerned about this, there are many online resources available to challenge it. Use the search terms 'online bullying' or 'online abuse' to research these, and try to talk to someone if you feel this is an issue for you.

8. Imagine you are employed as a security adviser for an international company. What advice would you give the directors in terms of potential cyberthreats and how to protect against them?

___

What new things have you learned?
What had you not thought about before?

Global health, food and well-being

> **Objective**
>
> **GI9.3E** – Awareness of the impact of some farming practices on animal welfare, land degradation, biodiversity and species and habitat loss.

> **We will learn:**
>
> - how farming practices affect animal welfare and the environment
> - examples where farming practices can reduce **environmental impacts**
> - examples where farming practices can improve animal welfare
> - how traditional farming practices can be adapted to modern farming.

> **Key vocabulary**
>
> agrochemicals, animal welfare, biodiversity, cover crops, direct sowing, environmental impacts, farming practices, habitats, intercropping, mechanisation, rotation cropping

> In the USA during the early 1930s, a combination of economic, farming and weather factors caused the 'Dust Bowl'. The landscape was overfarmed as the demand for wheat caused every available piece of land to be ploughed, including the prairie grass that held the soil together. Persistent high winds stripped the soil away, causing devastation.
>
> In this session, you will explore farming practice and the impacts it can have on biodiversity, habitats and animal welfare.

Global health, food and well-being: Session 5

Farming impacts on the soil, plants and animals. These impacts can be intentional or unintentional. Some impacts are positive, but many are negative, leading to a loss of biodiversity as **habitats** are damaged, sometimes beyond repair.

1 Draw lines to link the **farming practices** with their effects.

Use of insecticides	Can lead to rapid soil loss as the soil-binding roots are removed.
Land clearance (for example, deforestation) to create new farmland	Growing tomatoes out of season, for example, may need expensive climate control systems such as glasshouses. This removes the natural habitat completely.
Mechanisation of farming using large machinery	Spraying crops or treating seeds to kill certain insects often kills all the insects, not just the target species.
Use of nitrate fertiliser	Growing just one type of crop reduces the biodiversity gained from growing a variety.
Demand for all-year-round vegetables and fruit	Chemicals to control weeds often kill beneficial plants that are important for soil health and biodiversity.
Use of herbicides	Hedgerows and other boundaries are removed to create large, regular fields, resulting in loss of habitats.
Specialisation, for example, 'monoculture' (single type of crop)	Chemicals to promote growth can be washed into rivers and streams, causing pollution.

Global health, food and well-being: Session 5

Hydroponics (growing without soil) and climate-controlled systems (for example, glasshouse cultivation) can largely ignore naturally occurring soils. However, most agriculture depends on a healthy, fertile soil.

Soil is a combination of organic and inorganic material with its own fungi, plant and animal ecosystems. Naturally occurring soils can take hundreds of years to form, but this essential part of the farming landscape can be destroyed quickly if treated without thought.

2 Choose the correct words to complete the text below about soil.

waterlogging	problems	critical	loss
health	heavy	equilibrium	fungi
harm	insecticides	habitat	Soil

_____ is created from underground rocks weathering to form essential minerals that are then processed by plants, _____, insects and other animals. This will create a naturally occurring substance to support plant life and a _____ that is balanced, or in _____.

Farming practices can upset this equilibrium. **Agrochemicals** – including herbicides, fungicides and _____ – will affect the soil and may cause _____ to organisms that are _____ for good soil _____.

The use of _____ machinery can damage the structure of the soil, affecting drainage and causing _____. Removing vegetation to create new fields can lead to rapid erosion and soil _____.

Most farmers recognise the importance of the soil and take steps to improve and maintain its condition. However, not all do, and this causes long-lasting _____.

Global health, food and well-being: Session 5

Mechanisation of farming has occurred ever since machines were available. There has been a trend towards the use of increasingly large and heavy machines, which can carry out their purpose faster and more efficiently. This has had a significant impact on the farming landscape.

3 Look at the statements below regarding the use of farm machinery and decide whether they are true or false.

Statement	True or false?
Large machinery works just as well in small fields as it does in large fields.	
The weight of heavy machinery can damage the soil by compressing it and squeezing out the air spaces that are essential for good drainage.	
Smaller machines can pull just as big a plough as a large machine, so there is little advantage to using a large machine.	
Flotation tyres, caterpillar treads and dual rear tyres are sometimes used to reduce pressure on the soil, which results in less damage from soil compaction.	
Many small fields have had to be made larger for bigger machines to be used. This has caused a loss of habitats as field boundaries have been removed.	
Modern tractors use global positioning systems to guide the operator so that fields are tended more efficiently.	
It is better to use machinery across a slope rather than up and down the slope because it reduces rainwater run-off and erosion.	
Some farmers have stopped ploughing altogether and plant new crops straight into the remains of the previous, harvested crop. This is better for the environment.	
Farmers are experimenting with removing machinery altogether and tending even the largest fields by hand.	
Farmers are experimenting with using 'autonomous', or robot, machinery. This means they will make significant savings by not having the expense of a person to operate the machine.	

Obviously, growing plants, particularly crops, is one of the key purposes of a farming system. The choice of crop, the treatments needed and the method of cultivation will all have an impact on the environment.

In addition, farmers may also consider growing plants that are not directly commercial but may benefit the system as a whole.

4 Look at the notes below and, on the opposite page, design a poster or infographic that explains the factors affecting the growth of crops and other plants. Use the three headings listed below. Most of the notes are self-explanatory, but you might need to research some of the terms to make sure you understand them.

| Choice of crop | Crop treatment | Method of cultivation |

Choice of crop:
- Food, fuel (biofuels) or animal fodder? If food is needed, then are the others wasteful?
- Use of **cover crops** to restore soil fertility, reducing the need for expensive and environmentally damaging fertilisers
- Use of habitat-specific plants – for example, hedgerows, wild flowers – to improve **biodiversity**
- Crops suitable for the changing climate, for example, drought-resistant

Crop treatment:
- The fewer agrochemicals, the better it is for the environment
- Use of organic fertilisers instead of nitrates
- Use of spot treatment to minimise effect on non-target species

Method of cultivation (growing):
- **Rotation cropping** to replace nutrients
- **Direct sowing** (no ploughing), which maintains better soil health
- **Intercropping**, which improves biodiversity by growing different types of crop in the same field
- Planting trees to reduce wind erosion of the soil
- Use of machinery only when suitable, for example, not during heavy or prolonged rainfall

Global health, food and well-being: Session 5 — 197

Having read the notes on the opposite page, design your poster or infographic in the space below.

5 **Animal welfare** is a contentious issue for many people. We all make choices about the food we eat and farmers make choices about the food they produce. Look at the opinions below and then answer the questions that follow.

Elijah
I don't have much money to feed my family. I certainly don't want to pay more than I can afford. I trust the supermarket to make sure the animals are well treated. I don't see why we can't have good, cheap food and good animal welfare.

Josefa
I think the way farmed animals are treated is dreadful. Chickens jammed into cages that are too small. Wholesale use of antibiotics to keep away disease because the conditions they are kept in are appalling. That's why I don't eat meat.

Bea
I prefer to buy free-range meat and dairy products. I appreciate it costs farmers more to produce good-quality food with good animal welfare. It may cost a bit more to buy but we don't eat meat every day.

Amit
Consumers need to stop buying meat from countries that don't have high standards. I raise chickens in regulation cages with plenty of space and they can go outside. I wouldn't want to cut standards but high standards cost more. The supermarkets drive prices down and I end up barely covering my costs. It is hard to compete with cheap imports.

1 Which of the four views do you most agree with? Why?
   _____
   _____
   _____

2 Which of the four views do you least agree with? Why?
   _____
   _____
   _____

3 Explain whether or not you think it is possible to have cheap, good-quality food that is produced to high animal welfare standards.
   _____
   _____
   _____
   _____

In many countries, farmers are adopting and adapting traditional farming practices to provide solutions for modern-day problems. These problems include:

- overdependency on agrochemicals
- loss of biodiversity and habitats
- climate change.

Below are some examples of where traditional or indigenous farming technologies are being used to combat problems.

- The Green Hope Fund – Amazonian Rainforest
- The Permaculture Institute – Ghana
- The Soils, Food and Healthy Communities agroecology project – Malawi
- The National Hedgelaying Society – United Kingdom
- Fire-stick farming – Australia

6 Research **one** of the examples above (or choose one of your own) and, in the space below, explain how traditional farming techniques can still be relevant today.

_____
_____
_____
_____
_____
_____
_____
_____
_____
_____
_____
_____

200 Global health, food and well-being: Session 5

In this session, you have explored some of the issues facing farming and have seen that economic pressures to produce food can compromise biodiversity and habitats and cause long-lasting damage.

New advances in modern farming technology can reduce the impact, but there is also a place for more traditional or indigenous technologies and skills.

Farming has a great responsibility to maintain or improve animal welfare and environmental standards. Many farmers meet this challenge and regard themselves as stewards of the land. Consumers also have their part to play by understanding the challenges of modern farming and thinking carefully about where their food comes from.

7 Choose a habitat and draw a diagram showing how farming practices can cause damage to that ecosystem.

What new things have you learned?
What had you not thought about before?

Understanding rights

> **Objective**
>
> **HR9.5A** – Be familiar with a range of human rights treaties and conventions designed to protect people's rights and freedoms.

We will learn:

- what human rights are
- why we need protected rights
- how rights are protected
- how rights can be controversial.

Key vocabulary

arbitrary detention, charter, convention, declaration, sanctions, violations

Human rights is a subject that causes considerable argument. It seems reasonable that every person should have basic rights or freedoms to allow them to live peacefully without fear, but this is not the case. There are millions of people who do not share in the knowledge that their rights will be protected and that they are safe from rights abuses.

You may have heard of countries that have a 'poor record on rights', but what does this mean for the people living in those countries? What does it mean for other countries who may have strong economic, cultural or military links with those countries?

These are some of the issues you will explore in this session and which may lead you to question whether rights are a luxury or a necessity.

Throughout history, the way one person treats another or how a monarch, clan, government or tribe treats its people has been the subject of debate. Sometimes wars have been fought or armed insurrection has occurred in order to ensure the rights of the people are recognised and protected.

When Cyrus conquered Babylon in 539 BCE, his first act was to free the slaves and pass laws protecting freedom of religion and racial equality. This was recorded on a clay cylinder – the Cyrus Cylinder.

Recently, it has become more common for international organisations to find agreement between nation states and produce a **declaration** or **charter** of rights. All the countries concerned agree to uphold this charter and make sure they incorporate the principles into their own justice systems to give those rights a legal status for the protection of the people.

Understanding rights: Session 1

1 Draw lines linking various charters to their descriptions.

United States Declaration of Independence (1776)	Established the national government of the USA and the highest form of law, guaranteeing basic rights.
Constitution of the United States (1787)	The main international rights charter. Signed just after the Second World War and adopted by most countries since then.
Bill of Rights (1791)	The first of several conventions to govern how wars should be fought and how people should be treated.
Declaration of the Rights of Man and of the Citizen (1789)	When the USA declared independence, the document contained two main sections covering rights and the right to revolution.
The Geneva **Convention** (1864)	When France became a republic, this document laid out people's basic rights.
The Universal Declaration of Human Rights (1948)	The first 10 amendments to the Constitution of the United States, which protect, among other things, freedom of speech.
European Convention on Human Rights (1950)	Rights charters are not just the product of the Western world. This charter was drawn up by the African Union.
African Charter on Human and Peoples' Rights (1981)	This regional convention protects the rights of people who have endured years of total war.

Understanding rights: Session 1

2 What specific rights are referred to when we say that a country has a 'poor record' on rights? Choose the correct words to complete the text. Then answer the question below.

privacy	poor	monitored	critical

arrested	fair	speech	denial

Although there is a wide variety of rights, those countries with a _____ record target specific rights.

Freedom of _____ is commonly abused; many governments will not allow their people to say anything that is _____ of the way they are ruled.

The right to a _____ trial is also denied many people, who are often subject to another abuse: _____ of freedom from '**arbitrary detention**'. This means they are _____ but don't know why.

Finally, people should expect a right to _____ but this is often abused, and they are _____ , in person or online, for evidence of crimes against the state.

Why do countries that have agreed to follow, for example, the Universal Declaration of Human Rights, think it is acceptable to deny some of those basic rights to their citizens?

_____
_____
_____
_____
_____
_____

One dilemma facing countries is how to respond to nation states that have a poor rights record.

There may be close ties that mean a government is reluctant to condemn the behaviour of a nation state with a poor record. Some governments believe that maintaining close ties and engaging with an offending state is more effective than isolating them. Others believe that a range of **sanctions**, including cutting diplomatic and economic ties, is the only way to effect change.

3 Imagine you are going to debate the following statement:

It is better to engage with a nation state with a poor rights record than to condemn them.

Using notes or bullet points, add your arguments for and against this statement to the table below. Consider what motives a country might have to engage or condemn. For example, do arms sales, oil revenues and military alliances form part of the argument? Does any special relationship with the country mean change is more likely by engaging with them?

Aim for approximately an equal number of arguments for and against the statement.

Arguments for statement	Arguments against statement

Understanding rights: Session 1

> Over 160 countries are being monitored or have been reported for rights **violations**. Various organisations carry out this monitoring and reporting, including:
>
> - Amnesty International
> - Human Rights Watch
> - Civil Rights Defenders
> - Human Rights Without Frontiers
> - Human Rights Foundation

4 Research a country that has a poor rights record and produce a case study, in the form of a poster or infographic, on the opposite page.

Search the organisations mentioned above (or others) for examples and use the notes below to guide your research and the content you might include in your poster or infographic.

- Select and research a country that features in news items.
- Look for named people that have had their rights abused.
- Are there images or graphics you can include?
- A country that has a poor rights record will usually have concerns raised about more than one right, for example, detention without trial and inhumane treatment.
- State censorship of internet use or the introduction of martial law can indicate that a country might disregard certain rights.
- Is there a pattern, or something held in common, by those affected? A profile of a typical person affected could be useful.

1 Use the box below to make some of your own notes.

2 Having researched a country that has a poor rights record, now produce your case study, in the form of a poster or infographic, in the space below.

Understanding rights: Session 1

> While it may seem simple to agree that rights are a good thing, all sorts of contradictions emerge that often end up with the justice system making a ruling.

5 Look at the statements below and mark whether you agree or disagree with them. If you agree with a statement, place a tick next to it; if you disagree, place a cross. Then answer the questions on the opposite page.

Statement	✓ ✗
Freedom of speech means other people have the right to offend you by what they say.	
Some rights are more important than others. These take precedence over 'lesser' rights.	
Criminals do not have the same rights as other people. If they are suspects or are planning a crime, they forfeit their rights.	
Nation states have a duty to protect themselves, and if that means some people have to lose their rights, then that's a small price to pay.	
If you have done nothing wrong, then you have nothing to fear. People should remember this.	
Freedom of speech means it's okay to lie about someone and they can't do anything about it.	
Rights are so important that nothing or no one should be allowed to take them away.	
Nation states should be allowed to collect as much data and information about people as they need or want. It helps them make better decisions and keep everyone safe.	
When rights conflict with each other, there has to be a 'greater good' argument where one right is upheld over another for the common good.	

Understanding rights: Session 1   209

1. What kind of contradiction between different rights might mean the justice system having to make a judgement?

2. Why shouldn't the school bully be allowed the freedom to say hurtful things that cause upset for their victims?

3. Is it right that prisoners are deprived of their right to freedom and privacy? Explain your answer.

210 Understanding rights: Session 1

In this session, you have seen that the introduction of rights charters and conventions is often linked to human events, particularly wars or revolutions. You have discovered that while upholding rights should be a straightforward matter, it becomes more complex where international relations are concerned.

The very nature of rights can be controversial, and conflicting rights sometimes means that the justice system is needed to resolve disputes.

6 Select a piece of rights legislation and explain how it protects people's rights and freedoms. Use examples to illustrate your answer.

_____
_____
_____
_____
_____
_____
_____
_____
_____
_____
_____
_____
_____
_____
_____
_____

What new things have you learned?
What had you not thought about before?

Violation of rights

Human Rights   211

> **Objective**
>
> **HR9.5B** – Knowledge about the role of the United Nations in tackling the violation of rights globally.

We will learn:

- about common rights violations
- what is meant by a 'crime against humanity'
- how the United Nations and other organisations intervene.

Key vocabulary

crimes against humanity, genocide, resolution, war crimes

> **i** Throughout history, countries have carried out systematic repression of their population for ideological or political reasons.
>
> In this session, you will examine what is meant by a crime against humanity and the organisations that investigate these and hold individuals and countries to account for their actions.

Violation of rights: Session 2

Crimes against humanity are similar, but not to be confused with, **genocide** or **war crimes**. The term 'crimes against humanity' is relatively recent, although the historical record proves they have been committed for hundreds of years.

1 Select the correct words to complete the text.

| humanity | physical | genocide | policy |

| combatants | group | civilian |

Crimes against humanity occur when serious _____ or mental acts are systematically and knowingly carried out against a _____ population.

Genocide is when there is intentional destruction of a national, ethnic or religious _____.

War crimes are when, during a declared war, the 'rules of war' are broken by individuals against enemy _____ or civilians.

Crimes against _____ differ from genocide in that they are crimes committed against any civilian population regardless of ethnicity or beliefs.

War crimes differ from _____ or crimes against humanity in that they are committed by individuals rather than through any state _____.

There is clearly an overlap between these, particularly between genocide and crimes against humanity, which both systematically and knowingly target civilians.

Violation of rights: Session 2

How are crimes against humanity challenged? What can be done to bring criminals to account? The answer is complicated.

Legally, crimes against humanity, genocide and war crimes can be pursued without a time limit. This means that even for crimes committed 10, 20, 50 or more years ago, the perpetrators can still be held to account.

2 Look at the reasons below that some individuals, groups or nation states might give for not legally pursuing crimes against humanity, genocide or war crimes. In each case, give a reason why you believe these crimes should be legally challenged.

Reason not to challenge	Reason to challenge
Those committing such crimes believe their acts are justified and are an unfortunate part of conflict.	
It may need months, if not years, of painstaking research to apportion blame for a single incident.	
There will be allied nation states who will not want an investigation because of their own contribution or support for the perpetrators, and will block any attempt at one.	
History is written by winners. States or individuals who commit these crimes usually believe they will win and will write history to reflect this.	
Nation states or individuals engaged in crimes will just deny they happened, and after a few years they will be forgotten.	

There are organisations that investigate genocide, war crimes and crimes against humanity and hold those responsible to account.

- Foremost is the United Nations and its International Court of Justice. This court provides legal redress for humanitarian crimes.
- There are various human rights organisations that also investigate these crimes. You explored some of these in the previous session, 'Understanding rights'.
- Governments, mainstream media and investigative organisations also carry out research to provide evidence of crimes.

The question is: how effective are these organisations in combating humanitarian crimes?

3 Read the speech bubbles below and decide where you think the best chance of conviction lies by answering the questions on the opposite page.

United Nations: We have identified individuals that may be guilty of war crimes. We need witnesses to come forward and testify.

Government agency: We have satellite imagery that we believe shows civilian populations being targeted and provides possible proof of crimes against humanity.

Mainstream media: We have obtained photographs and eyewitness accounts of what we think is genocide taking place.

Investigative research organisation: We have military recordings, global positioning references, photographs and videos that show the nation state knew they were targeting air strikes against schools and hospitals.

1. Which of the views expressed opposite do you think provides the most reliable evidence of a humanitarian crime being committed? Why?

   _____
   _____
   _____
   _____
   _____

2. With limited resources, which organisation would you support to find conclusive evidence? Why?

   _____
   _____
   _____
   _____
   _____

3. What would be the most reliable additional evidence you would require to conclusively prove, for all concerned (even those involved), that a humanitarian crime had been committed?

   _____
   _____
   _____
   _____
   _____

The United Nations is the organisation that most people think of when humanitarian crimes are suspected. "Why doesn't the United Nations do something about it?" is the question often asked.

The reason why is, simply, that the United Nations functions on consensus. That is, it can only directly intervene in a conflict, through peacemaking or peacekeeping operations, if ALL the nation states involved agree. Otherwise they cannot intervene. That's the problem.

4 Using the information above, and your own research, answer the questions below.

1 Why might a nation state object to a United Nations **resolution** giving authority for direct military action against another state suspected of humanitarian crimes?

_____
_____
_____
_____
_____

2 Should the United Nations be able to intervene without the consent of all the factions involved if humanitarian crimes are suspected? Explain your answer.

_____
_____
_____
_____
_____

3 The United Nations relies on military forces being 'loaned' by other nations. Do you think it should have its own military forces, independent of any other nation? Explain your answer.

_____
_____
_____
_____
_____

It is not the United Nations that brings those suspected of humanitarian crimes to justice. It is the International Criminal Court (ICC) that investigates and, where warranted, tries individuals charged with the gravest crimes of concern to the international community: genocide, war crimes, crimes against humanity and the crime of aggression.

Again, though, the ICC can only act on evidence brought before it. It has no powers to intervene where humanitarian crimes are suspected.

5 Outline what system you would put in place to:
- intervene to stop humanitarian crimes being committed
- bring to justice those suspected of humanitarian crimes.

_____
_____
_____
_____
_____
_____
_____
_____
_____
_____
_____
_____
_____
_____
_____
_____
_____
_____

Violation of rights: Session 2

In this session, you have seen that what should be a straightforward goal is far more complex. There is no doubt that humanitarian crimes – including genocide, war crimes and crimes against humanity – are a daily occurrence. Most people would agree that these are not the mark of a civilised global community.

However, there seem to be barriers both to preventing these crimes and also to bringing those responsible to justice. Collaboration to stop, investigate and bring to justice the perpetrators of such crimes is often obstructed.

Progress has been made but it may need a more determined effort, from governmental and non-governmental organisations, to significantly reduce the suffering that these crimes cause.

6 Explain, using an example, what constitutes a crime against humanity.

_____
_____
_____
_____
_____

7 What role does the United Nations take in tackling the violation of rights?

_____
_____
_____
_____
_____

What new things have you learned?
What had you not thought about before?

Refugees, asylum seekers and internally displaced people

> **Objective**
>
> **HR9.5C** – Find out about refugees, asylum seekers and internally displaced people in their locality and act to support them.

We will learn:

- who refugees, asylum seekers and internally displaced people are
- about the scale of the issue and why there is such a problem
- about the support that people need and the organisations that help
- what you can do.

Key vocabulary

asylum seeker, forcibly displaced person, internally displaced person, migrant, refugee, United Nations High Commissioner for Refugees (UNHCR)

ⓘ By the beginning of 2020, the United Nations High Commissioner for Refugees (UNHCR) estimated there were nearly 80 million forcibly displaced people across the world. Most concerning is that this number has almost doubled since 1990 and would still seem to be increasing.

In this session, you will explore why there is such a crisis and what can be done to challenge the problem and help those concerned.

It was only in relatively recent history, from the eighteenth and nineteenth centuries, that what we understand as nations came to be recognised and people were defined partly by their citizenship of a nation or country. This meant that people forced to flee their country became stateless, and '**refugee**' became a recognised term.

1 Select the correct words to complete the text. Then answer the questions opposite.

| discrimination | unskilled | wealthy | UNHCR | natural | war |

| protection | migrant | forced | remains | country | origin |

The main difference between a _____ and a **forcibly displaced person** is that a migrant usually chooses to move, while a forcibly displaced person is _____ to move.

A **refugee** is defined as someone who has fled violence, _____ , conflict or persecution and has crossed an international boundary to find safety in another _____ . All refugees are initially asylum seekers.

An **asylum seeker** is someone seeking international _____ , who has made a claim for, but has not yet been granted, the status of refugee. Not all asylum seekers will become recognised as refugees and some may be returned to their country of _____ .

An **internally displaced person** is someone who flees their home because of armed conflict or _____ or human disaster but who _____ within their country.

A **migrant** is not defined by the _____ . A migrant most usually chooses to move to another country and might be _____ , poor, professional or _____ . It is a term used mainly by the media to describe all people who move from one country to another, but is confusing and often leads to _____ against those seeking sanctuary.

1 Should refugees be regarded the same as migrants? Explain your answer.

_____
_____
_____
_____
_____

2 Why do you think many mainstream media often refer to migrants when they should refer to refugees seeking protection?

_____
_____
_____
_____
_____

3 Why do you think some countries are reluctant to offer protection to refugees?

_____
_____
_____
_____
_____

The number of refugees has increased dramatically over the past ten years. People flee their homes because they fear for their safety. So what are they fleeing from?

Many people flee their homes because of natural or human disaster. For example, in Bangladesh, over 200,000 people leave their homes each year because of river flooding. Many may return once the floods subside, but they are part of the 25 million people each year who are displaced by natural disasters. Over 350,000 people had to be permanently resettled after the Chernobyl nuclear disaster in 1986. In both these cases, and in most natural or human disasters, the people are 'internally displaced': they remain within their country and are not recognised as refugees.

Those that flee to another country are refugees, and the main cause is conflict.

To understand the scale of the problem, look at the table below. This lists the ten countries with the highest numbers of refugees.

Country	Number of refugees	Shade	% of population
Lebanon	1,500,000	Dark	22
Jordan	1,000,000	Dark	11
Turkey	4,300,000	Medium	5
Liberia	230,000	Medium	5
Uganda	1,700,000	Medium	4
Sudan	1,000,000	Medium	3
Germany	1,200,000	Light	2
Bangladesh	675,000	Light	1
Ethiopia	1,000,000	Light	1
Kenya	470,000	Light	1

Refugees, asylum seekers and internally displaced people: Session 3 — 223

2 Shade the map below. Use a single colour and shade the countries dark, medium or light according to the information in the table on the opposite page. Then answer the questions that follow.

1. Notice that the shade reflects the number of migrants as a percentage of the population of the host country. Why is this more significant than the actual number of refugees?

   _____
   _____
   _____
   _____

2. Describe the distribution of refugees as shown on the map.

   _____
   _____
   _____
   _____

Refugees, asylum seekers and internally displaced people: Session 3

> Refugees often flee with little more than the clothes they are wearing and what few possessions they can carry. Read Yacob's story.
>
> "My peaceful life came to an end the day the soldiers arrived and our house got burnt. The houses in our village were all on fire. We couldn't run to the jungle because it was on fire, too. We fled to another village but that village was also attacked. We were stranded, so we fled again, to a canal, and stayed there for two days with no food. We made it across the border and now we live here in the camp.
>
> We have no papers, no money – just the clothes we wear. There are thousands of us in the camp. I don't know how long we will be here. I don't know what has happened to the rest of my family.
>
> I would like to leave the camp but I have nowhere to go and I can't go back home."

3 Imagine you are Yacob. Complete the table below to show what help and support you might need, and to explain why it is needed.

My needs	Why I need this

4 You have looked at areas with a high percentage of refugees, and you may live in or near a region that has a large refugee population.

In this activity, you should investigate refugees in your area, to find out what they need and to see what you could do to help. For example, sometimes refugees want to tell their story. Could you invite a refugee to address your class or interview them for a school magazine? They may need help learning a language or making appointments with officials. Perhaps they need help accessing the internet.

Use the boxes below to outline the situation and the help you might be able to give.

Description of refugees in my local area

The support that is needed

I could...

In the previous activities, you considered what help and support is needed to meet the needs of refugees. But what support do the countries that give them shelter need? You saw earlier that Lebanon shelters 1,500,000 refugees, which accounts for over 20 per cent of its total population. Consider how much support Lebanon needs to meet the basic needs of its refugee population.

5   In Activity 6, you are going to write a letter to the heads of state of other countries, requesting assistance in the refugee situation affecting your country.

In preparation for this, research the **United Nations High Commissioner for Refugees (UNHCR)** and other organisations that support refugees. Look also at other countries that you think might be able to help.

Make notes on your research in the box below.

6 Using your research from Activity 5, write your letter to be sent to the heads of state of other countries, in which you:

1. remind them of their obligations towards refugees

2. request short- and long-term assistance in dealing with the refugee situation affecting your country, outlining the reasons for such support.

Write your letter in the space below.

In this session, you have explored some of the issues surrounding refugees. It is a situation that most of us will never experience, but it is a very real situation for an increasing number of people.

Refugees are stateless. They cannot go home because they left in fear of their lives. Other countries have a legal and moral obligation to protect and care for them. Often refugees are discriminated against as if, somehow, it is 'their fault'. As you should now understand, nobody would willingly become a refugee, and we as individuals have a responsibility to help them. They are people who by circumstance, not design, need the support of others to rebuild their lives.

7 Design a poster to show how people can support refugees, asylum seekers and internally displaced people in your local area.

What new things have you learned?
What had you not thought about before?

Human rights defenders

> **Objective**
>
> **HR9.5D** – Imagine what a community where everyone has their rights protected could look like.

> **We will learn:**
> - which human rights need defending
> - how they should be defended
> - whether a world in which all rights are protected is really possible.

> **Key vocabulary**
>
> protected rights, utopia

i In literature, there are many examples of novels describing life in an 'ideal' world or community. Sir Thomas More was the first writer, in 1516, to describe a perfect imaginary world in which people share a common culture and way of life. His book was entitled *Utopia*.

The creation of such an ideal world or utopia is, as many would argue, only possible in fiction – real-world examples do not exist. However, in India, the USA, Denmark and a few other countries, communities have been created, with varying degrees of success, where rights and freedoms are respected. These communities may provide lessons that could benefit the world at large.

This session asks you to imagine a community in which the rights of all are protected. Is this utopia possible? Would individual freedoms have to be sacrificed to protect the rights of all? And how would those rights be protected?

Human rights defenders: Session 4

1 Complete the table by listing those rights you would ensure are protected within your utopian community and those you think should not be protected.

You should review examples of **protected rights** by looking at, for instance, the United States Constitution and Bill of Rights, and the Universal Declaration of Human Rights.

Also look at the rights protected in your own region or country for some ideas.

Once you have completed the table, answer the question below.

Protected rights

Non-protected rights

1 Should people in your imaginary utopian community be able to choose which rights they will uphold and protect, and which they will ignore? Explain your answer.

_____
_____
_____
_____

Human rights defenders: Session 4   **231**

The extent to which people will uphold rights will depend on a number of factors. These include:

- the nature of the society
- the benefits of living in a community with protected rights
- the characteristics of the people
- the laws or controls that ensure rights are protected.

2 Look at the statements below and decide whether you agree or disagree with them. If you agree with a statement, place a tick next to it; if you disagree, place a cross.

You could think also about topics you may already have studied, for example, systems of government or economics. Look also at some examples by researching 'Utopian communities that exist' or 'How many communities live a utopian life?'.

Statement	✓ ✗
The community can only protect all rights if all the people think the same way.	
The people have to be carefully chosen. You can't just hope that the people already living there will agree. It has to be a new community.	
There has to be a leader, with a council, to ensure that people know who to follow.	
People will need to live and work together. There can't be too many individuals living separate lives to everybody else.	
There will have to be special courts to examine situations where one person claims someone has abused the rights of another person.	
People will need to be paid the same so that everyone is equal, even though they may do different jobs.	
The main benefit of living in such a community is the freedom to do what you like without having to follow rules that are there to control you.	
A community where rights are protected will be free from crime, hate and envy – every single person will be treated equally.	
In a community where rights are protected, people who succeed will do so because of who they are and not because they come from a privileged background.	
The main problem is going to be stopping people from outside trying to join the community. Not everyone will be suitable.	

3 The table below lists some of the questions that need to be addressed when designing a community in which all rights are protected. Complete the table by adding your own questions and ideas. Use bullet points or notes. Some examples are included for the first one.

Questions to consider	Ideas and further questions
How will society be organised?	- Will it be a collective? - Will it be a commune where people live and work together? - Will people follow their own lives and just live in the community?
What type of people would want to live in such a community?	
What would be the main benefits of living in such a community?	
What procedures would need to be put in place to ensure rights are protected?	

4 You should now have a good idea of what your community should look like and how it should function. Now it is time to recruit people to join you!

In the box below, design a recruitment advertisement to explain what type of people you are looking for and to persuade them to apply.

5 Imagine your community has been running for a year. Has it succeeded? Have you created a wondrous **utopia**?

In the space below, write two short diary entries. The first is a celebration of success: your community has thrived, rights are protected and people are safe, happy and fulfilled. The second is a reflection on why it did not succeed. Where did it go wrong?

When you have written both diary entries, answer the question below.

One year on – we have succeeded ☺

One year on – we have not succeeded ☹

Which of your diary entries is more likely? Why?

_____
_____
_____
_____
_____

In this session, you have imagined your own community where rights are protected, and looked at some of the factors and issues that would need to be considered. Those issues are the same as those that are faced in the 'real world' wherever rights are threatened.

Everyone has a right to be treated fairly and equally, both in the sight of other people and in law. Achieving this is often difficult – but that is not a reason for not attempting it.

6 Write a press release to announce the 'opening' of your community and explaining what life will be like.

_____
_____
_____
_____
_____
_____
_____
_____
_____
_____
_____
_____
_____
_____

What new things have you learned?
What had you not thought about before?

Good governance

> **Objective**
>
> **PG9.6A** – Understand how countries and organisations around the world collaborate to tackle global challenges and injustices such as terrorism.

> **We will learn:**
>
> - what global challenges and injustices there are
> - what global and international collaboration means
> - why global collaboration is required to tackle challenges and injustices
> - how collaboration is achieved.

> **Key vocabulary**
>
> collaboration, global collaboration, global crime, international collaboration, people smuggling, people trafficking

i The world is a complex place. For example, the movement of food, manufactured goods and people takes place locally, nationally and internationally. This requires complicated interactions to work properly, considering both the people involved and their physical and political environments.

These movements and interactions drive global economic and social systems on which we all depend. These systems, in turn, need to be well managed to ensure they work correctly.

Unfortunately, either deliberately or through ignorance, there are individuals and organisations who look for opportunities to exploit these systems for profit or power: criminal organisations smuggle people and drugs; large corporations cause major pollution incidents; governments conspire with and against one another for political or economic gain. All of these create global challenges and injustices that no one person or organisation can successfully overcome. They can be addressed only if people collaborate with one another.

1 There are many global challenges or injustices that create serious problems. Select the correct words to complete the text that describe some of these.

unpaid	asylum	smuggling	girls
social	persecuted	human right	economic
slavery	religious	refugees	governments

People trafficking: This is different from people _____ in many respects. People trafficking involves people, particularly women and _____, being moved by force or deception and pushed into modern-day _____. This is low-paid or _____ work, often in dangerous and abusive jobs.

Persecution: There has recently been a rapid global increase in the number of people or groups of people being _____ because of their _____ beliefs or ethnicity. In some cases, this appears to be condoned or even carried out by government forces. This has led to huge increases in people seeking _____ in other countries.

Refugee protection: The right to seek asylum (safety or protection) is a basic _____. However, asylum seekers may be denied access to regions that consider _____ to be a threat for _____, _____ or security reasons. However, the United Nations Refugee Agency is working to guide _____ to respect international refugee law.

238 Good governance: Session 1

Of the many global challenges that the world faces, this activity will focus on two specific areas:

- Drugs
- **People smuggling**

One of the main organisations combating **global crime** is the United Nations Office on Drugs and Crime (UNODC).

2 Research the following two documents produced by the UNODC.

- **UNODC 2020 World Drug Report – Press Release**: this provides information on trends in global drug use
- **Global Study on Smuggling of Migrants (GLOSOM) 2018 – Executive Summary**: this provides information on the smuggling of migrants

Use the information to produce an infographic on the opposite page on **either** global drug use **or** people smuggling. Research other sources for information to add to your infographic, which should include:

- the causes that have led to the problem
- statistics, facts or figures that show the scale of the problem and whether it is increasing, decreasing or remaining consistent.

Use the box below to make any notes.

Use this page to produce your infographic on **either** global drug use **or** people smuggling.

Good governance: Session 1

> Phrases that are typically used when talking about how to combat many of the issues raised in this session include:
>
> - 'A global effort is needed...'
> - 'Governments must work together...'
> - 'An inter-agency approach is essential...'
>
> In other words, there needs to be **collaboration**: people and organisations need to work together to tackle a particular issue. This collaboration happens on a variety of different levels and scales.

3 Look at the organisations listed in the table below, which all work collaboratively to tackle environmental issues.

Complete the table to show whether the name of each organisation suggests it operates internationally, nationally or regionally. Then research each organisation and, in the last column, add the name of at least one other organisation with which it collaborates.

Organisation	How it operates	Who it collaborates with
London Air Quality Network		
Terra Conscious, India		
Global Ecolabelling Network		
International Institute for Environment and Development		
Singapore Environment Council		
China Environmental United Certification Center		

At first glance, you might see just a hierarchy of organisations listed in Activity 3, with the different types simply covering greater or smaller regions. However, these organisations are woven together by collaboration.

For example, the Singapore Environment Council collaborates with the China Environmental United Certification Center through a 'memorandum of understanding', and both are members of the Global Ecolabelling Network. This links them to other regional and national organisations in Southeast Asia, North Asia, East Asia, North America and Europe, all of which collaborate with the aim of ecological protection.

This shows that regional organisations have a big part to play in global change.

4 Using the box below, show the connections between the regional, national and international organisations described in the example above in the form of a flow diagram of your own design.

Regional, national and international organisations collaborate with each other because of the nature of the challenges they face. One challenge is how countries deal with policing their borders, to prevent the entry of illegal immigrants.

Look at the maps below. The first map shows routes taken by migrants entering the EU illegally in 2014–2015. The second map shows the movement of migrants (not only illegal immigrants) to and through Europe during the first half of 2015. The maps do not show the migrants' countries of origin.

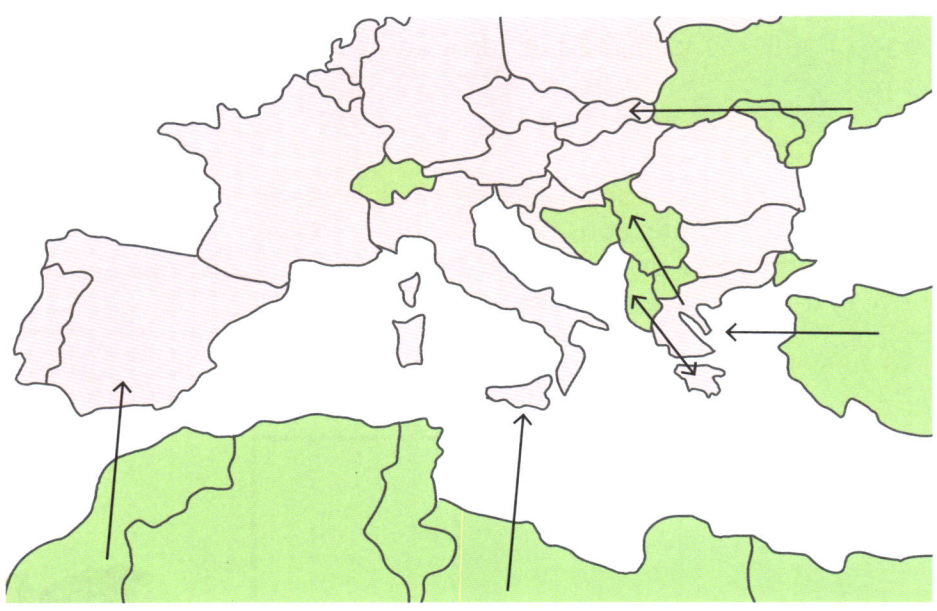

EU Countries   Non EU Countries

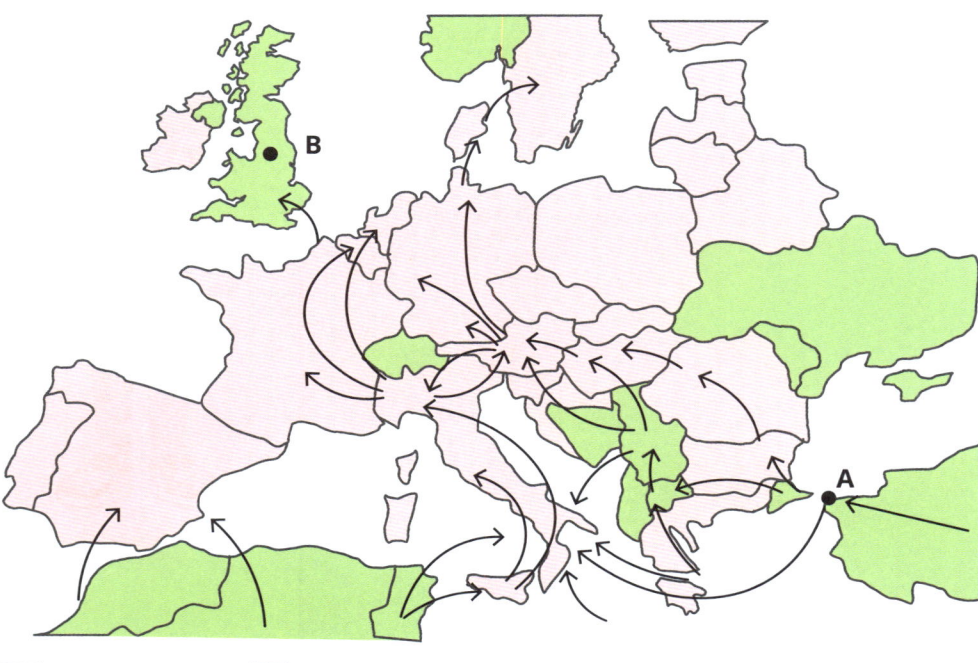

EU Countries   Non EU Countries

> **5** Answer the following questions using information from the maps on the opposite page.

1. Look at the first map. How many points of entry into the European Union does it show there are for illegal migrants? Why might this pose a problem for countries trying to police their borders?

   _____
   _____
   _____

2. Look at the second map. What modes of transport could be used by immigrants going to and through the European Union? Why might this pose a problem for policing illegal immigration?

   _____
   _____
   _____

3. Look at the second map. How many countries would a migrant need to travel through to get from point A to point B? What effect do you think this could have on policing illegal immigration?

   _____
   _____
   _____

4. Why might the answers to the questions above mean organisations in the European Union have to collaborate?

   _____
   _____
   _____

5. What different roles do you think regional, national and international organisations may have within this collaboration? Make suggestions rather than researching examples.

   Regional: _____
   _____

   National: _____
   _____

   International: _____
   _____

6 Think about the factors that (a) promote and (b) hinder effective collaboration between individuals, organisations and countries. Then complete the statements below. The first one has been done for you as an example.

The direct seriousness of the threat:

a) Some countries might regard the threat very seriously and will want as much assistance as possible as it affects them directly.

b) Others might not see it as important and will be reluctant to be involved as they are not directly affected.

The cost of collaboration:

a) _____

b) _____

The need to share sensitive information:

a) _____

b) _____

The knowledge or skills needed:

a) _____

b) _____

The way collaboration will be managed:

a) _____

b) _____

Good governance: Session 1   245

Activity 6 showed that tackling global challenges and injustices may provide opportunities but also barriers for collaboration. Ideally, effective collaboration takes place when certain conditions are met.

7 Draw lines to link each of the five headings from Activity 6 with a strategy that could produce effective collaboration.

The direct seriousness of the threat	The resources needed will be reasonable or pooled so the wealthier countries pay more.
The cost of collaboration	Relevant research and specialist organisations will be shared as needed.
The need to share sensitive information	Control and command is collective, and organisations' independence is maintained.
The knowledge or skills needed	Only sensitive information relating to the threat will need to be shared.
The way collaboration will be managed	There is a shared or common challenge that affects everyone.

Good governance: Session 1

> Collaboration is about persuading people and organisations to join together to meet a challenge. Sometimes collaboration reveals hidden concerns that need to be understood and addressed.

8 Imagine you are the head of an organisation that has been created to combat a serious global criminal threat. At the first meeting, the members from different organisations ask the questions shown below.

On the next page, give an understanding answer to each question that should reassure the questioner. Question 1 has been completed for you, as an example.

Question 1
We will target just this specific challenge, won't we?

Question 2
How do we know working together will overcome this challenge?

Question 3
This isn't going to affect our relations with other countries, is it?

Question 4
We won't be doing anything illegal, will we?

Question 5
How can I justify this to the government and the people of my country?

Question 6
How will we deal with any disagreements?

Question 1

Answer: We have clear boundaries that define where our efforts will be focused.

Question 2

Answer: _____
_____
_____
_____
_____

Question 3

Answer: _____
_____
_____
_____
_____

Question 4

Answer: _____
_____
_____
_____
_____

Question 5

Answer: _____
_____
_____
_____
_____

Question 6

Answer: _____
_____
_____
_____
_____

> You have explored some of the major global challenges and injustices that affect us, and seen that some require global or **international collaboration** if they are to be addressed. You have also seen what collaboration means, and some of the factors that make collaboration effective.

9 Research **one** global challenge and, in the space below, outline the challenge and assess whether you think the organisations involved have collaborated effectively. You could choose any of the challenges you have explored, or a different one that interests you.

_____
_____
_____
_____
_____
_____
_____
_____
_____
_____
_____
_____
_____
_____
_____
_____
_____
_____
_____
_____

Good governance: Session 1   **249**

In this session, you have seen how some global challenges can be tackled only by working collaboratively. You have looked at:

- examples of global challenges
- what collaboration means and why it is needed
- ways in which agencies and countries collaborate
- some possible barriers to collaboration.

Global challenges need global solutions. No single individual, organisation or country has the resources to solve these problems. Working together, though, can make a difference.

10 In the box below, design a logo to promote **global collaboration** that highlights the benefits of this approach.

What new things have you learned?
What had you not thought about before?

Participation and inclusion (Greater Depth)

Power and Governance

Objective

PG9.6B – Desire to work collaboratively on a project to increase inclusion and challenge unfair practices.

We will learn:

- what it means to increase inclusion and challenge unfair practices
- how to decide on a project to achieve this
- what records to keep
- how to evaluate the project and your contribution.

Key vocabulary

evaluation criteria, inclusion, Occam's razor, process evaluation, product evaluation, project brief, unfair practices

In the previous session, you explored how some challenges are best tackled collaboratively – in other words, working with other people or organisations to achieve a common goal.

In this session, you will investigate and carry out or take part in a project that has the aims of increasing inclusion and challenging unfair practices. You will devise ways of recording your involvement in the project and its progress. Finally, you will look at ways of analysing the success of the project and your contribution.

Your project should have the following three goals or aims.

1. **It must involve you working collaboratively**. You could join an existing project run by an organisation and take part in the activities they provide. Or you could start your own project to address an issue that you find particularly interesting. Either way, you should ensure that you are working with others as part of a team.

2. **It must promote inclusion**. This means that you identify people or groups of people that are usually excluded for one reason or another. Maybe their views are not heard, or they are prevented from taking part in activities or opportunities open to others.

3. **It must also challenge unfair practices**. This means that the reasons people are being excluded from participating or having the opportunities to participate are unjust or represent some form of inequality.

This is called the '**project brief**'. It is important to fully understand the project brief so that you keep on track. If you are unsure, then ask for help.

1 Look at the list of possible projects below, and put a tick next to those you think meet **all** the aims above and a cross next to those that do not.

- ☐ You write a letter to your local government officer complaining that one of their workers left a full recycling bin when they were last emptied.
- ☐ You and some friends campaign to provide equal sporting opportunities for girls at your school.
- ☐ You join a lunchtime or after school chess club.
- ☐ You become student coordinator for a UNICEF school-based campaign to improve education in Somalia.
- ☐ You make a video showing rundown or derelict areas in your community and suggesting what could be done to improve them.

When choosing your project, you should consider the following questions.

- Does it meet your project brief's three main aims as outlined on the previous page?
- Is it something that interests you?
- Can you afford the time, commitment and, possibly, money to see the project through?
- Who can help you? Who will be in your team?
- Is there a school project you could contribute to?
- Are there official campaigns run by reputable organisations that would welcome your help?

Once you have a good idea what your project will be, try explaining it to friends, teachers or parents, and see what they think. Explaining it to others will help you order your thoughts, and you might find their advice useful.

Once you have finally decided what to do, think about publicising your intentions. Is there a social media group connected to the project that you could join?

2 In the space below, write a summary of your chosen project. Once you have finished, check that it will meet the project brief and that it is something you will enjoy doing.

_____
_____
_____
_____
_____
_____
_____

Keeping a record of your project and your involvement in it is important. It will help you keep on track and ensure your planning is carried out efficiently.

Projects can vary greatly but, in general, there are things that should be considered:

- **What planning is needed?** Do things have to happen at a certain time or in a particular order? Make use of timelines, flow charts, calendars, 'to do' lists or other tools to ensure you know you are on target and haven't overlooked something. Think about going through these records with someone else to get their opinion or suggestions. Search online for 'how to run a school project' for ideas.

- **Keep a diary.** This could be a video diary or a more traditional written record. If you are submitting your project file as part of an assessment, a diary will be essential.

- **Make sure you have people to help you.** Your project needs to be collaborative, so you need to work as part of a team. Choose people whose skills complement yours. Are you good at ideas but not so good on detail? Then you need a 'detail' person. Do you need artwork for posters? A photographer? There will be students, friends and family who can help.

- **Keep reminding yourself of the aims.** If you find yourself planning activities that do not seem to relate to the aims, you may have got sidetracked and will need to refocus.

- **Remember the other demands on your time.** Learn to balance your time. Search online for 'good time-management skills' for advice on how to do this.

- **Record the things that go wrong, not just those that go well**. Famously, Thomas Edison said – after 10,000 failed attempts at making a working, reliable light bulb – "I have not failed. I have just found 10,000 ways that won't work!"

- **Keep a project file.** If all your planning, organisation, contacts and other details are in one place, you won't waste time or get frustrated trying to find things. If a lot of your work is IT generated, make sure you have copies or backups. Try to keep important documents, pictures or scans in 'cloud storage' so you can access them from anywhere.

- **Hold regular review meetings with your team**. For an extended project, this will ensure that everyone continues to work to the common goal.

3 In the space below, list **five** methods you will use to record or manage your project. You can include some of the suggestions above – but try to think of some of your own.

1 _____
2 _____
3 _____
4 _____
5 _____

It will be unusual if, during your project, there are no problems and everything goes as planned. There are always problems. Good planning and management will avoid many problems; the ones left will need to be solved. Good problem-solving skills will help with those.

Look at the flow chart below. It shows one way of problem solving.

Step 1: Understand the problem

Sometimes people jump straight to a solution without really knowing what the problem is – or even if there is a problem! Explaining what you think is the problem to someone else is a good way of checking that you know what the problem is.

Step 2: Understand any limitations

Will solving the problem cost anything? How much time is there to come up with a solution? Can you solve the problem or does it need someone with different skills?

Step 3: Think of solutions

Try to think of more than one solution, unless the solution is obvious. If you cannot think of solutions, ask other people to help.

Step 4: Choose a solution

Be guided in this by '**Occam's razor**' (also known as the 'law of parsimony'). This states that 'the simplest solution is usually the best'. In other words, try to avoid an over-complicated solution – the more complicated the solution, the more things there are that can go wrong!

Step 5: Implement the solution

Carry out the solution, but be mindful that you may need to make adjustments. If the adjustments are too radical or significantly affect other areas, the solution is probably not the correct one and you may not have a full understanding of the problem.

Step 6: Evaluate the solution

Did it work? If so, move on – but check that your solution hasn't caused a knock-on effect somewhere else. If the solution didn't solve the problem, then consider firstly, has the problem gone away? It does sometimes happen that what you think is a problem turns out not to be. If there is still a problem, go back to Step 1, but definitely think about getting help.

Participation and inclusion: Session 2

4 A group has decided that their project to promote inclusion and challenge unfair practices is going to take the form of an evening musical performance in the school hall. During the course of the project however, the group encounters a number of problems.

For each problem below, work your way through steps 2, 3 and 4 of the flow chart on the opposite page to decide on the best solution. Make notes to record your ideas and indicate your chosen solution by underlining or highlighting it.

Problem 1: A number of the performers are unable to make the final, important rehearsal the evening before the actual performance.

_____
_____
_____
_____
_____
_____

Problem 2: After the first rehearsal, it is obvious that the performance will be 10 minutes too long.

_____
_____
_____
_____
_____
_____

Problem 3: The lead vocalist loses her voice a week before the performance.

_____
_____
_____
_____
_____
_____

Whilst you will instinctively sense how well (or otherwise) your project has gone, a formal evaluation allows you to keep a longer-lasting record of this and will help you get the most out of the experience. If you are submitting your project for assessment, a formal evaluation will be an essential requirement.

There are several ways of carrying out a formal evaluation. These are the most common:

- **Self evaluation**. You carry this out yourself and no one else is involved.
- **Peer evaluation**. Other students, who may or may not have been involved in the project, carry it out with you.
- **Tutor evaluation**. Your teacher or another adult carries it out with you.

5 Think of an advantage and a disadvantage for each type of evaluation above and add these to the table.

Type of evaluation	Advantage	Disadvantage
Self evaluation		
Peer evaluation		
Tutor evaluation		

It is common to use a combination or self, peer and tutor evaluation. Doing this means that you should maximise the advantages of each method while avoiding most of the disadvantages. However you decide to evaluate the project, though, there are two important aspects that must be included.

- **You must evaluate the project itself ('product evaluation')**. For example: You decided to produce a web page for an online school magazine to raise awareness of the plight of child soldiers. This is the 'product' and must be evaluated.
- **You must also evaluate the process ('process evaluation')**. This is mainly concerned with evaluating how well you and your team worked together to progress the project and produce the product.

To evaluate both product and process, you need to decide on the '**evaluation criteria**' – that is, what specifically you will examine to assess how successful the product and process have been. The simplest criteria are produced using 'SWOT analysis'. SWOT looks at:

- **S**trengths – what went well, achieving what was expected?
- **W**eaknesses – what didn't go so well?
- **O**pportunities – how could the weaknesses be improved or the strengths developed?
- **T**argets – what was done and by when?

6 Look at the following evaluation questions that might be asked in relation to the online child soldier example mentioned above. Indicate whether you think these evaluate the product or the process.

Evaluation question	Product or process?
Did all the online links work?	
How well did we work as a team?	
Was the project clearly concerned with inclusion and challenging unfair practices?	
Did I contribute fully?	
Did we meet all the deadlines?	
Should more images or graphics have been included?	
How could I improve my problem-solving skills?	
Did people find the web page informative?	

In this session, you have explored how to run a project and some of the issues that involves. You have looked at:

- how to understand what the project brief means
- what to consider when choosing a project
- how to record progress and your contribution
- the need to evaluate both the product and the process.

One of the most important things to remember is that people will help you, but you have to ask!

7 What are your top **five** tips for working as part of a team? Present these in the form of a poster in the space below.

What new things have you learned?
What had you not thought about before?

Glossary

absolute poverty – not having enough income or material possessions to meet basic human needs

agrochemicals – chemicals used in farming (for example, herbicides, fertilisers, fungicides, pesticides)

analyse – to examine or think about something carefully, in order to understand it

animal welfare – the physical and mental well-being of animals, for example, in relation to their living conditions and how they are treated

arbitrary detention – imprisonment or confinement without just cause

armed conflict – armed groups, countries or states engaging in military operations against each other

arms trade – the buying and selling of military equipment and technology

asylum seeker – person who leaves their own country because they are in danger, especially for political reasons, and who asks the government of another country to allow them to live there

Atlantic slave trade – the buying (or abducting) and selling of African men, women and children to provide free labour for European colonisers, particularly on the American continent during the sixteenth to nineteenth centuries

attributes – the natural physical qualities or features of a person, for example, hair colour

behaviours – the things a person does

biodiversity – the variety of plants and animals in a particular place

biomes – types of environment that are described according to the typical weather conditions and plants that exist there, for example, a rainforest

Black Lives Matter (BLM) – a social justice movement protesting against racially motivated violence against Black people and more general racial inequalities

Boston Square – a tool to help pritoritise tasks

bug-out bag – a rucksack containing supplies to help you cope in an emergency

carbon credits – permission to produce particular amounts of carbon dioxide, which companies and individuals can buy and sell as a way of reducing harm to the environment

charter – a statement of the principles, duties and purposes of an organisation

climate change – a permanent change in planet Earth's weather conditions

Cold War – the unfriendly relationship between the United States and the Soviet Union after the Second World War

collaboration – when you work together with another person or group to achieve something

colonisation – the process of establishing political control over an area or over another country, and sending your citizens there to settle

conflict resolution – the process of bringing to an end disputes between armed groups, countries or states through peaceful means

convention – a formal agreement, especially between countries, about particular rules or behaviour

cover crops – crops grown to improve the soil

crimes against humanity – a crime of cruelty against large numbers of people, especially in a war

criminal activity – doing things that are illegal

criteria – standards used to judge something or make a decision about something

cyberwarfare – acts of aggression carried out by one country against another country using the internet

decision matrix – a research tool to help you make a decision based on specified alternatives and criteria

declaration – an important official statement about a particular situation or plan

defence – all the systems, people, materials, and so on that a country uses to protect itself from attack

direct sowing – planting crops without the use of a plough to better maintain the health of the soil

direct discrimination – treating one person or group differently specifically because of that person or group's protected characteristic (for example, age, disability, religion)

indirect discrimination – when a person or group is disadvantaged by a general policy or rule intended to treat people in the same way

discrimination – the practice of treating one person or group differently from another in an unfair way

disinformation – false information that is given deliberately in order to hide the truth or confuse people, especially in political situations

economic system – the particular way in which the economy of a country is organised, for example, whether the economy is controlled by the government or allowed to develop in its own way

environmental impact – the (usually negative) effects of something on the environment

equality – when all people are treated in the same way and have the same opportunities

ethical entrepreneurship – starting or running a business with the goal of improving the world, rather than just for profit

evaluate – to judge how good, useful or successful something is

evaluation criteria – standards used to judge how good, useful or successful something is

extreme climate event – a natural event, such as a hurricane or heatwave, that has a serious impact on a particular area's environment and animal and human populations

fact checking – the process of confirming that a stated fact is actually true

fake news – news deliberately intended to deceive, especially for political purposes

farming practices – things done by farmers to produce their goods; these can have positive or negative effects on land or animals

First Nation – a name given specifically to some indigenous peoples of Canada

flow diagram – a drawing that uses shapes and lines to show how the different stages in a process are connected to each other

food insecurity – not being able to produce enough food to sustain a community, for example, because of short- or long-term environmental impacts on crops

forcibly displaced person – a person who is forced to move from their home or their local area

genocide – the deliberate murder of a whole group of people, sometimes of the same ethnicity

global arms sales – the buying and selling of military equipment around the world

global collaboration – when people around the world work together to achieve something

global connectivity – the ability of computers and other electronic equipment to connect with the internet or with other computers or programs around the world

global crime – illegal activities that take place across national borders and are not restricted to a particular region, for example, people trafficking and drugs smuggling

global inequalities – unfair situations around the world in which some groups in society have more money, opportunities, power, and so on than others

global initiatives – new plans or processes to achieve particular aims or to solve particular problems around the world

Global North – a term used to describe the wealthiest and most industrialised countries of the world, most of which are in the northern hemisphere

Global South – a term used to describe the poorest

Glossary

and least industrialised countries of the world, most of which are in the southern hemisphere

habitat – the natural home of a plant or animal

harassment – treating someone in a hostile, humiliating or degrading way because of their protected characteristic (for example, age, disability, ethnicity)

hurricane – a storm that has very strong, fast winds and that moves over water

identity – the qualities and attitudes that a person or group of people have that make them different from other people

inclusion – the act of including someone or something in a larger group or set, or the fact of being included in one

indigenous – people or things that have always been in the place where they are, rather than being brought there from somewhere else

inequality – an unfair situation in which some groups in society have more money, opportunities, power, and so on than others

injustice – a situation in which people are treated very unfairly and not given their rights

institutionalised racism – a form of racism perpetuated through the established rules and/or practices of a society or organisation

intercropping – growing different crops in the same field to improve biodiversity

internally displaced person – someone who is forced to leave a local area or region (especially during a war, or for political or religious reasons) but who remains within the borders of their home country

international collaboration – working together with people or groups from different countries to achieve something

internet (data) cables – wires that enable computers to access the internet

market forces – the way that the behaviour of buyers and sellers affects the levels of prices and wages, without any influence from the government

mechanisation – the process of using machines instead of people or animals to carry out tasks

micro-aggression – a small difference in choice of word or attitude that reveals a hidden prejudice

micro-discrimination – hidden prejudice revealed by a small difference in choice of word or attitude

migrant – someone who goes to live in another area or country, especially in order to find work

military equipment – tools, machines, and so on used by an army, navy or air force

misinformation – incorrect information, especially when deliberately intended to deceive people

modal node – the place where two or more types of transport meet, for example, a train station at an airport

mode of transport – a particular way of moving people or things (for example, car, ship)

neonicotinoids – an insecticide used to kill aphids or grubs in the soil by coating seeds or spraying plants

net zero carbon emissions – a term used to describe the goal of removing as much carbon dioxide from the atmosphere as is released into the atmosphere

network – a set of computers that are connected to each other so that they can share information

news organisations – companies that collect and distribute news stories

Occam's razor – the principle which states that the simplest, least complicated explanation is usually the best

parasites – plants or animals that live on or in another plant or animal and get food from it

peacebuilding – creating or maintaining peace through non-military means, for example, by introducing measures to improve aspects of society in the affected region (for example, schools, healthcare)

peacekeeping – creating or maintaining a truce between armed groups, countries or states, often through the use of military personnel from countries not involved in the conflict or United Nations peacekeepers

people smuggling – illegally moving people from one country to another with their consent

people trafficking – illegally moving people from one country to another without their consent, usually to profit from their labour

phishing – the criminal activity of sending emails or having a website that is intended to trick someone into giving away personal information such as their bank account number or their computer password. This information is then used to get money or goods

plant reproduction – the creation of offspring by plants

plantation – a large area of land in a hot country, where crops such as tea, cotton and sugar are grown

pollinator – an animal that gives a flower or plant pollen so that it can produce seeds

poverty line – the minimum level of income below which someone is considered to be poor

prejudice – an unreasonable dislike and distrust of people who are different from you in some way, especially because of their ethnicity, sex, religion, for example; used to show disapproval

private company – company that does not offer shares for sale on the stock exchange

process evaluation – a way of judging how well or successfully something was achieved; that is, the actions taken to achieve something, not the end product itself

product evaluation – a way of judging how good, useful or successful something is in comparison to what was intended

project brief – a short description of the aims and methods of a project written at the start of a project

protected characteristics – nine elements of people's identity that it is illegal to disciminate against in the United Kingdom (including age, disability, ethnicity, religion)

protected rights – rights (for example, freedom of speech) that are protected by law

public company – company that offers shares for sale to the public on the stock exchange

public health – the health and well-being of the population as a whole

ransomware – computer software designed to block access to a computer system until money (ransom) is paid

refugee – someone who has been forced to leave their country, especially during a conflict, or for political or religious reasons

relative poverty – having an income 60 per cent below the median household income

reliability – the consistency of, for example, a news article, indicating how far it can be trusted

research (noun) – study of a subject in order to discover new facts or test new ideas

research (verb) – to study a subject in detail, especially in order to discover new facts or test new ideas

resolution – a formal decision or statement agreed on by a group of people, especially after a vote

resource portfolio – a system of files/folders to store and organise resources, for example, for a project

reverse search – a way of searching for information about something on the internet using the thing itself in the search, for example, using an image to search for information about the image (who created it, where it appears on the internet, and so on)

rotation cropping – growing different crops in a field, one after another to keep the soil healthy

sanctions – forms of diplomatic or economic punishment that can be used if a country disobeys a rule or law

scamming – tricking someone out of something, usually money

scoping – researching a project at the beginning to find out what is relevant and what is worth including or discarding

security – things that are done to keep a person, building or country safe from danger or crime

self-esteem – the feeling of being satisfied with your own abilities, and that you deserve to be liked or respected

sense of self – an understanding of your own identity

SMART targets – a way of setting targets that are specific (S), measurable (M), attainable or achievable (A), related or realistic (R) and time-limited (T)

social justice – the idea that everyone should have equal rights and equality of opportunity regardless of, for example, ethnicity, gender, religion

social media – ways of sharing information, opinions, images, videos and such like using the internet, especially social networking sites

statistics – numbers that represent facts or measurements

storm surge – the rising of sea water in response to a storm

street gang – a group of young people who spend time together in public places, who are often involved in crime or drugs and who often fight against other groups

sustainable – able to continue without causing damage to the environment

Sustainable Development Goals (SDGs) – goals set up by the United Nations to achieve a better world

synthesise – to combine separate things into a complete whole

systemic inequalities – inequalities faced by particular people or groups that are the result of general unfairness within society, for example, a particular social group lacking equal access to healthcare or education

technology – machines, equipment and ways of doing things that are based on modern knowledge about science and computers

telecommunications – the sending and receiving of messages by telephone, computer, radio, television and so on

TRAFFIC – the Wildlife Trade Monitoring Network

transport system – all the elements needed to move people and goods around, how these elements interact and how they are organised (for example, trains, rail tracks, train stations, rail timetables)

Triangular Trade – the three-way movement of goods, raw materials and enslaved people associated with the Atlantic slave trade

tropical storm – a storm originating from or happening in the hottest parts of the world

unfair practices – things that are done which unjustly exclude certain people from participating

United Nations High Commissioner for Refugees (UNHCR) – the United Nations agency responsible for helping refugees and internally displaced and stateless people

United Nations Office on Drugs and Crime (UNODC) – a United Nations office whose aim is to make the world safer from drugs, crime, terrorism and corruption

utopia – an imaginary perfect world where everyone is happy

validity – the accuracy of, for example, a news article, indicating how far it can be trusted

victimisation – the unfair or cruel treatment of someone because they made a compaint relating to discrimination

violations – actions that break a law, agreement, principle and such like

war – fighting between two or more countries or between opposing groups within a country, involving large numbers of soldiers and weapons

war crime – a cruel act done during a conflict which is illegal under international law

wildfire – a fire that moves quickly and cannot be controlled

wildlife – animals and plants growing in natural conditions

World Wide Web – the system for making information available, anywhere in the world, to computer users who are connected to the internet

worldview – someone's opinions and attitudes relating to the world and things in general